Johann Wolfgang von Goethe

FAUST

The German Library: Volume 18

Volkmar Sander, General Editor

Johann Wolfgang von Goethe

FAUST

Parts 1 and 2

Edited by Victor Lange

CONTINUUM · NEW YORK

1994

The Continuum Publishing Company
370 Lexington Avenue, New York, NY 10017

The German Library
is published in cooperation with Deutsches Haus,
New York University.
This volume has been supported by Inter Nationes, and a grant
from Deutsches Haus.

Printed in the United States of America

Library of Congress Cataloging-in-Publication Data

Goethe, Johann Wolfgang von, 1749–1832.
    [Faust. English]
    Faust. Parts 1 and 2 / Johann Wolfgang von Goethe ; edited by
Victor Lange ; [translated by Louis MacNeice].
        p.   cm. — (The German library ; v. 18)
    ISBN 0-8264-0724-2 (acid-free paper) — ISBN
0-8264-0725-0 (pbk. : acid-free paper)
    I. Lange, Victor, 1908–   . II. Title. III. Series.
PT2026.F2M3   1994
832'.6—dc20   93-6287
                                                                              CIP

Contents

Translated by Louis MacNeice

Introduction

1

It is axiomatic that the great historical figures of any society represent in their mythological elaboration greatness as well as failure, pride as well as humility, faith and deception. In few of the poems that have represented the lives of such figures is this dichotomy rendered so powerfully and dramatically as it is in Goethe's *Faust*.

The life of the historical personage of Johann Faust, born presumably in 1480, is documented as that of a medical and theological scholar, but also as a soothsayer and performer at market fairs. In the memory of his contemporaries Faust was a figure of remarkable learning and as such, suspect of being in league with supernatural beings. He died about 1540, already the object of curiosity and of admiration for his desire, like Paracelsus, to gain a comprehensive understanding of the universe. Some forty years after his death, in 1587, a speculative biography, the *Historia von D. Johann Fausten,* describes the life of a scholar who is determined, in league with the devil, to transcend the limits of human knowledge, to discover the structure and function of the elements. This extravagant and un-Christian aspiration Faust regrets at the end, the devil carries him off, and the reader of the booklet is warned against sacrilegious transgressions.

The story of Doctor Faust exercised an incomparable appeal: Christopher Marlowe wrote between 1587 and 1593 a play, the text of which produced a variety of theatrical entertainments, the most popular of which was the puppet play that Goethe saw as a boy in Frankfurt. He used this as the core of his earliest attempt at a more complex rendering of the triangular relationship between Faust, Mephistopheles, and Margaret. This first version, the *Urfaust* (written about 1770), in its form disjointed and sketchy, deals with only two aspects of the story: Faust the scholar, and Faust the lover of Margaret, the two themes intertwined as examples of the extravagance of human aspirations for total knowledge and total love.

Not until 1788, during his Italian journey, did Goethe add further scenes. He reflected on the possibility of elaborating the "Helena" motif and thus of transcending the "northern" world by moving the action to Greece. The "second part" is committed throughout to the poetic resources of the classical imagination and presents, through the active presence of Mephistopheles, an ironic view of modern archaeology and philology.

The second part of *Faust* was begun before the first was completed; he added, rearranged, and modified constantly. In 1800 Goethe read a significant section of the second part to his friend Schiller who called it a "synthesis of the noble and the barbarous." But it was not until Easter 1808 that *Faust, The first part of the Tragedy* appeared, introduced by a "Prologue in Heaven" that touches on themes of the second part. The complete work, *Faust I and II,* that had preoccupied him for some sixty years, was finally published in 1832, shortly after Goethe's death. The selections of our edition indicate something of the mosaic character of the composition.

2

Whatever the intellectual and poetic coherence of *Faust* as a whole may be, it is not a work of carefully calculated design. The two parts are not in every respect interdependent. Much of the first part reflects the "titanic" spiritual ambitions of a magus of the Renaissance. Faust's association with the God-subordinated "devil" Mephistopheles is counterbalanced with his emerging passion for the simple and entirely humane figure of Margaret. These two strands produce the dramatic tension of the first part.

The second part is far more complex in its figures and problems: here Faust is primarily the searcher for the classical embodiment of perfection as represented by Helena. After her death his striving for the assertion of the self in grandiose and noble social plans is ironically defeated by Mephistopheles; Faust dies and, without resolving the ethical ambiguities of his career, he is taken into the divine company—of whom Margaret is one—to be forgiven.

The conflict in Faust of superhuman ambitions both spiritual and political and, therefore, the challenge to the established Christian faith is at the core of the play; it represents the key to Faust's career and motivates several of the incidents woven into the plot. Faust's love for Margaret has the double function of a total commitment to human attachment and in the end, through Mephistopheles' command, the diabolical abandonment of that love.

In the second part, Faust's passion for Margaret is no longer a central issue; nor is the function of Mephistopheles essentially so demonic and destructive as it is in the first. Faust, determined to find the ultimate reality of beauty in Helena, the classical idol in the intensity of romantic perception, finds himself in the skeptical company of Mephistopheles, a modern visitor of ancient mythological constellations. He is in the end confronted by his own hubris and dies in anticipation of that highest degree of being that has been his supreme, if at times ruthless, ambition. He is forgiven for his transgressions in a succession of religious metaphors, for which his ceaseless "striving" offers the poetic justification.

3

Of the many English translations of *Faust,* the editors have chosen a version by the Irish poet Louis MacNeice who, in cooperation with the distinguished Oxford Germanist, Ernest Stahl, produced the text for a 1949 commemorative BBC broadcast on the occasion of the 200th anniversary of Goethe's birth. This is in many ways an experiment that demanded concession in length and a selection in the cast of figures that, the editors felt, gave to a venerable text a freshness of perspective and a poetic flavor that no other translation has achieved. That the substance of Goethe's monumental drama has in this translation been preserved and enhanced will be felt by all who know the poem in the original or another translation.

Even in a version as free and keyed to the special purpose of presenting a difficult text to radio listeners, the characteristic gestures of Goethe's prosody are maintained, and convey much of the musical and rhythmic quality of the original. As against the romantic character of such a widely admired Victorian translation as Bayard Taylor's, MacNeice and Stahl have chosen to remain close to the original German manner of poetic speech and have attempted to reproduce the lyrical as well as the intellectual qualities of the poem in a mode close to modern poetic sensibilities. They have indicated certain passages they felt could not be adequately accommodated in a lively modern rendering of this classic work; and while the legitimacy of the omission of certain scenes and figures may—and should—be argued by a critical reader, the effect of this English text as a whole is persuasive, faithful to Goethe's superb craftsmanship, and deeply moving.

V. L.

To
my great friend
E. L. STAHL
who went through the German text with me line by
line and without whom I should never have started,
let alone ended,
this translation

Louis MacNeice

FAUST

PART 1

PROLOGUE IN HEAVEN

The Lord. The Heavenly Hosts. Mephistopheles following

(The Three Archangels step forward)

RAPHAEL:

The chanting sun, as ever, rivals
The chanting of his brother spheres
And marches round his destined circuit—
A march that thunders in our ears.
His aspect cheers the Hosts of Heaven
Though what his essence none can say;
These inconceivable creations
Keep the high state of their first day.

GABRIEL:

And swift, with inconceivable swiftness,
The earth's full splendour rolls around,
Celestial radiance alternating
With a dread night too deep to sound;
The sea against the rocks' deep bases
Comes foaming up in far-flung force,
And rock and sea go whirling onward
In the swift spheres' eternal course.

MICHAEL:

And storms in rivalry are raging
From sea to land, from land to sea,
In frenzy forge the world a girdle
From which no inmost part is free.
The blight of lightning flaming yonder
Marks where the thunder-bolt will play;
And yet Thine envoys, Lord, revere
The gentle movement of Thy day.

CHOIR OF ANGELS:

Thine aspect cheers the Hosts of Heaven
Though what Thine essence none can say,

And all Thy loftiest creations
Keep the high state of their first day.

(*Enter Mephistopheles*)

MEPHISTOPHELES:

Since you, O Lord, once more approach and ask
If business down with us be light or heavy—
And in the past you've usually welcomed me—
That's why you see me also at your levee.
Excuse me, I can't manage lofty words—
Not though your whole court jeer and find me low;
My pathos certainly would make you laugh
Had you not left off laughing long ago.
Your suns and worlds mean nothing much to me;
How men torment themselves, that's all I see.
The little god of the world, one can't reshape, reshade him;
He is as strange to-day as that first day you made him.
His life would be not so bad, not quite,
Had you not granted him a gleam of Heaven's light;
He calls it Reason, uses it not the least
Except to be more beastly than any beast.
He seems to me—if your Honour does not mind—
Like a grasshopper—the long-legged kind—
That's always in flight and leaps as it flies along
And then in the grass strikes up its same old song.
I could only wish he confined himself to the grass!
He thrusts his nose into every filth, alas.

LORD:

Mephistopheles, have you no other news?
Do you always come here to accuse?
Is nothing ever right in your eyes on earth?

MEPHISTOPHELES:

No, Lord! I find things there as downright bad as ever.
I am sorry for men's days of dread and dearth;
Poor things, *my* wish to plague 'em isn't fervent.

LORD:

Do you know Faust?

MEPHISTOPHELES:
> The Doctor?

LORD:
> Aye, my servant.

MEPHISTOPHELES:
> Indeed! He serves you oddly enough, I think.
> The fool has no earthly habits in meat and drink.
> The ferment in him drives him wide and far,
> That he is mad he too has almost guessed;
> He demands of heaven each fairest star
> And of earth each highest joy and best,
> And all that is new and all that is far
> Can bring no calm to the deep-sea swell of his breast.

LORD:
> Now he may serve me only gropingly,
> Soon I shall lead him into the light.
> The gardener knows when the sapling first turns green
> That flowers and fruit will make the future bright.

MEPHISTOPHELES:
> What do you wager? You will lose him yet,
> Provided *you* give *me* permission
> To steer him gently the course I set.

LORD:
> So long as he walks the earth alive,
> So long you may try what enters your head;
> Men make mistakes as long as they strive.

MEPHISTOPHELES:
> I thank you for that; as regards the dead,
> The dead have never taken my fancy.
> I favour cheeks that are full and rosy-red;
> No corpse is welcome to my house;
> I work as the cat does with the mouse.

LORD:
> Very well; you have my full permission.
> Divert this soul from its primal source
> And carry it, if you can seize it,

Down with you upon your course—
And stand ashamed when you must needs admit:
A good man with his groping intuitions
Still knows the path that is true and fit.

MEPHISTOPHELES:

All right—but it won't last for long.
I'm not afraid my bet will turn out wrong.
And, if my aim prove true and strong,
Allow me to triumph wholeheartedly.
Dust shall be eat—and greedily—
Like my cousin the Snake renowned in tale and song.

LORD:

That too you are free to give a trial;
I have never hated the likes of you.
Of all the spirits of denial
The joker is the last that I eschew.
Man finds relaxation too attractive—
Too fond too soon of unconditional rest;
Which is why I am pleased to give him a companion
Who lures and thrusts and must, as devil, be active.
But ye, true sons of Heaven, it is your duty
To take your joy in the living wealth of beauty.
The changing Essence which ever works and lives
Wall you around with love, serene, secure!
And that which floats in flickering appearance
Fix ye it firm in thoughts that must endure.

CHOIR OF ANGELS:

Thine aspect cheers the Hosts of Heaven
Though what Thine essence none can say,
And all Thy loftiest creations
Keep the high state of their first day.

(*Heaven closes*)

MEPHISTOPHELES (*alone*):

I like to see the Old One now and then
And try to keep relations on the level.
It's really decent of so great a person
To talk so humanely even to the Devil.

The First Part of
the Tragedy

NIGHT

*(In a high-vaulted narrow Gothic room Faust, restless,
in a chair at his desk)*

FAUST:

Here stand I, ach, Philosophy
Behind me and Law and Medicine too
And, to my cost, Theology—
All these I have sweated through and through
And now you see me a poor fool
As wise as when I entered school!
They call me Master, they call me Doctor,
Ten years now I have dragged my college
Along by the nose through zig and zag
Through up and down and round and round
And this is all that I have found—
The impossibility of knowledge!
It is this that burns away my heart;
Of course I am cleverer than the quacks,
Than master and doctor, than clerk and priest,
I suffer no scruple or doubt in the least,
I have no qualms about devil or burning,
Which is just why all joy is torn from me,
I cannot presume to make use of my learning,
I cannot presume I could open my mind
To proselytize and improve mankind.

Besides, I have neither goods nor gold,
Neither reputation nor rank in the world;
No dog would choose to continue so!
Which is why I have given myself to Magic
To see if the Spirit may grant me to know
Through its force and its voice full many a secret,
May spare the sour sweat that I used to pour out
In talking of what I know nothing about,

May grant me to learn what it is that girds
The world together in its inmost being,
That the seeing its whole germination, the seeing
Its workings, may end my traffic in words.

O couldst thou, light of the full moon,
Look now thy last upon my pain,
Thou for whom I have sat belated
So many midnights here and waited
Till, over books and papers, thou
Didst shine, sad friend, upon my brow!
O could I but walk to and fro
On mountain heights in thy dear glow
Or float with spirits round mountain eyries
Or weave through fields thy glances glean
And freed from all miasmal theories
Bathe in thy dew and wash me clean!

Oh! Am I still stuck in this jail?
This God-damned dreary hole in the wall
Where even the lovely light of heaven
Breaks wanly through the painted panes!
Cooped up among these heaps of books
Gnawed by worms, coated with dust,
Round which to the top of the Gothic vault
A smoke-stained paper forms a crust.
Retorts and canisters lie pell-mell
And pyramids of instruments,
The junk of centuries, dense and mat—
Your world, man! World? They call it that!

And yet you ask why your poor heart
Cramped in your breast should feel such fear,
Why an unspecified misery
Should throw your life so out of gear?
Instead of the living natural world
For which God made all men his sons
You hold a reeking mouldering court
Among assorted skeletons.

Away! There is a world outside!
And this one book of mystic art
Which Nostradamus wrote himself,
Is this not adequate guard and guide?
By this you can tell the course of the stars,
By this, once Nature gives the word,
The soul begins to stir and dawn,
A spirit by a spirit heard.
In vain your barren studies here
Construe the signs of sanctity.
You Spirits, you are hovering near;
If you can hear me, answer me!

(*He opens the book and perceives the sign of the Macrocosm*)

Ha! What a river of wonder at this vision
Bursts upon all my senses in one flood!
And I feel young, the holy joy of life
Glows new, flows fresh, through nerve and blood!
Was it a god designed this hieroglyph to calm
The storm which but now raged inside me,
To pour upon my heart such balm,
And by some secret urge to guide me
Where all the powers of Nature stand unveiled around me?
Am I a God? It grows so light!
And through the clear-cut symbol on this page
My soul comes face to face with all creating Nature.
At last I understand the dictum of the sage:
'The spiritual world is always open,
Your mind is closed, your heart is dead;
Rise, young man, and plunge undaunted
Your earthly breast in the morning red.'

(*He contemplates the sign*)

Into one Whole how all things blend,
Function and live within each other!
Passing gold buckets to each other
How heavenly powers ascend, descend!
The odour of grace upon their wings,
They thrust from heaven through earthly things
And as all sing so *the* All sings!

What a fine show! Aye, but only a show!
Infinite Nature, where can I tap thy veins?
Where are thy breasts, those well-springs of all life
On which hang heaven and earth,
Towards which my dry breast strains?
They well up, they give drink, but I feel drought and dearth.

(*He turns the pages and perceives the sign of the Earth Spirit*)

How differently this new sign works upon me!
Thy sign, thou Spirit of the Earth, 'tis thine
And thou art nearer to me.
At once I feel my powers unfurled,
At once I glow as from new wine
And feel inspired to venture into the world,
To cope with the fortunes of earth benign or malign,
To enter the ring with the storm, to grapple and clinch,
To enter the jaws of the shipwreck and never flinch.
Over me comes a mist,
The moon muffles her light,
The lamp goes dark.
The air goes damp. Red beams flash
Around my head. There blows
A kind of a shudder down from the vault
And seizes on me.
It is thou must be hovering round me, come at my prayers!
Spirit, unveil thyself!
My heart, oh my heart, how it tears!
And how each and all of my senses
Seem burrowing upwards towards new light, new breath!
I feel my heart has surrendered, I have no more defences.
Come then! Come! Even if it prove my death!

(*He seizes the book and solemnly pronounces the sign of the
Earth Spirit. There is a flash of red flame and the Spirit
appears in it*)

SPIRIT:

Who calls upon me?

FAUST:

Appalling vision!

SPIRIT:

> You have long been sucking at my sphere,
> Now by main force you have drawn me here
> And now—

FAUST:

> No! Not to be endured!

SPIRIT:

> With prayers and with pantings you have procured
> The sight of my face and the sound of my voice—
> Now I am here. What a pitiable shivering
> Seizes the Superman. Where is the call of your soul?
> Where the breast which created a world in itself
> And carried and fostered it, swelling up, joyfully quivering,
> Raising itself to a level with Us, the Spirits?
> Where are you, Faust, whose voice rang out to me,
> Who with every nerve so thrust yourself upon me?
> Are you the thing that at a whiff of my breath
> Trembles throughout its living frame,
> A poor worm crawling off, askance, askew?

FAUST:

> Shall I yield to Thee, Thou shape of flame?
> I am Faust, I can hold my own with Thee.

SPIRIT:

> In the floods of life, in the storm of work,
> In ebb and flow,
> In warp and weft,
> Cradle and grave,
> An eternal sea,
> A changing patchwork,
> A glowing life,
> At the whirring loom of Time I weave
> The living clothes of the Deity.

FAUST:

> Thou who dost rove the wide world round,
> Busy Spirit, how near I feel to Thee!

SPIRIT:

> You are like that Spirit which you can grasp,
> Not me!

> (*The Spirit vanishes*)

FAUST:

> Not Thee!
> Whom then?
> I who am Godhead's image,
> Am I not even like Thee!

> (*A knocking on the door*)

> Death! I know who that is. My assistant!
> So ends my happiest, fairest hour.
> The crawling pedant must interrupt
> My visions at their fullest flower!

(*Wagner enters in dressing-gown and nightcap, a lamp in his hand*)

WAGNER:

> Excuse me but I heard your voice declaiming—
> A passage doubtless from those old Greek plays.
> That is an art from which I would gladly profit,
> It has its advantages nowadays.
> And I've often heard folk say it's true
> A preacher can learn something from an actor.

FAUST:

> Yes, when the preacher is an actor too;
> Which is a not uncommon factor.

WAGNER:

> Ah, when your study binds up your whole existence
> And you scarcely can see the world on a holiday
> Or through a spyglass—and always from a distance—
> How can your rhetoric make it walk your way?

FAUST:

> Unless you feel it, you cannot gallop it down,
> Unless it thrust up from your soul
> Forcing the hearts of all your audience
> With a primal joy beyond control.

Sit there for ever with scissors and paste!
Gather men's leavings for a rehash
And blow up a little paltry flicker
Out of your own little heap of ash!
It will win you claps from apes and toddlers—
Supposing your palate welcome such—
But heart can never awaken a spark in heart
Unless your own heart keep in touch.

WAGNER:

However, it is the delivery wins all ears
And I know that I am still far, too far, in arrears.

FAUST:

Win your effects by honest means,
Eschew the cap and bells of the fool!
True insight and true sense will make
Their point without the rhetoric school
And, given a thought that must be heard,
Is there such need to chase a word?
Yes, your so glittering purple patches
In which you make cat's cradles of humanity
Are like the foggy wind which whispers in the autumn
Through barren leaves—a fruitless vanity.

WAGNER:

Ah God, we know that art
Is long and short our life!
Often enough my analytical labours
Pester both brain and heart.
How hard it is to attain the means
By which one climbs to the fountain head;
Before a poor devil can reach the halfway house,
Like as not he is dead.

FAUST:

Your manuscript, is that your holy well
A draught of which for ever quenches thirst?
You have achieved no true refreshment
Unless you can tap your own soul first.

WAGNER:

Excuse me—it is considerable gratification
To transport oneself into the spirit of times past,
To observe what a wise man thought before our days
And how we now have brought his ideas to consummation.

FAUST:

Oh yes, consummated in heaven!
There is a book, my friend, and its seals are seven—
The times that have been put on the shelf.
Your so-called spirit of such times
Is at bottom merely the spirit of the gentry
In whom each time reflects itself,
And at that it often makes one weep
And at the first glance run away,
A lumber-room and a rubbish heap,
At best an heroic puppet play
With excellent pragmatical Buts and Yets
Such as are suitable to marionettes.

WAGNER:

And yet the world! The heart and spirit of men!
We all would wish to understand the same.

FAUST:

Yes, what is known as understanding—
But who dare call the child by his real name?
The few who have known anything about it,
Whose hearts unwisely overbrimmed and spake,
Who showed the mob their feelings and their visions,
Have ended on the cross or at the stake.
My friend, I beg you, the night is now far gone;
We must break off for this occasion.

WAGNER:

I'd have been happy sitting on and on
To continue such a learned conversation.
To-morrow however, as it is Easter Day,
I shall put you some further questions if I may.

Having given myself to knowledge heart and soul
I have a good share of it, now I would like the whole.

(Exit Wagner)

FAUST *(alone)*:

To think this head should still bring hope to birth
Sticking like glue to hackneyed rags and tags,
Delving with greedy hand for treasure
And glad when it finds an earthworm in the earth!

That such a human voice should here intrude
Where spiritual fulness only now enclosed me!
And yet, my God, you poorest of all the sons
Of earth, this time you have earned my gratitude.
For you have snatched me away from that despair
Which was ripe and ready to destroy my mind;
Beside that gigantic vision I could not find
My normal self; only a dwarf was there.

I, image of the Godhead, who deemed myself but now
On the brink of the mirror of eternal truth and seeing
My rapturous fill of the blaze of clearest Heaven,
Having stripped off my earthly being;
I, more than an angel, I whose boundless urge
To flow through Nature's veins and in the act of creation
To revel it like the gods—what a divination,
What an act of daring—and what an expiation!
One thundering word has swept me over the verge.

To boast myself thine equal I do not dare.
Granted I owned the power to draw thee down,
I lacked the power to hold thee there.
In that blest moment I felt myself,
Felt myself so small, so great;
Cruelly thou didst thrust me back
Into man's uncertain fate.
Who will teach me? What must I shun?
Or must I go where that impulse drives?
Alas, our very actions like our sufferings
Put a brake upon our lives.

Upon the highest concepts of the mind
There grows an alien and more alien mould;
When we have reached what in this world is good
That which is better is labelled a fraud, a blind.
What gave us life, feelings of highest worth,
Go dead amidst the madding crowds of earth.

Where once Imagination on daring wing
Reached out to the Eternal, full of hope,
Now, that the eddies of time have shipwrecked chance on
She is contented with a narrow scope.   [chance,
Care makes her nest forthwith in the heart's deep places,
And there contrives her secret sorrows,
Rocks herself restlessly, destroying rest and joy;
And always she is putting on new faces,
Will appear as your home, as those that you love within it,
As fire or water, poison or steel;
You tremble at every blow that you do not feel
And what you never lose you must weep for every minute.

I am not like the gods—that I too deeply feel—
No, I am like the worm that burrows through the dust
Which, as it keeps itself alive in the dust,
Is annulled and buried by some casual heel.

Is it not dust that on a thousand shelves
Narrows this high wall round me so?
The junk that with its thousandfold tawdriness
In this moth world keeps me so low?
Shall I find here what I require?
Read maybe in a thousand books how men
Have in the general run tortured themselves,
With but a lucky one now and then?
Why do you grin at me, you hollow skull?
To point out that your brain was once, like mine, confused
And looked for the easy day but in the difficult dusk,
Lusting for truth was led astray and abused?
You instruments, I know you are mocking me
With cog and crank and cylinder.
I stood at the door, you were to be the key;
A key with intricate wards—but the bolt declines to stir.

Mysterious in the light of day
Nature lets none unveil her; if she refuse
To make some revelation to your spirit
You cannot force her with levers and with screws.
You ancient gear I have never used, it is only
Because my father used you that I retain you.
You ancient scroll, you have been turning black
Since first the dim lamp smoked upon this desk to stain you.
Far better to have squandered the little I have
Than loaded with that little to stay sweating here.
Whatever legacy your fathers left you,
To own it you must earn it dear.
The thing that you fail to use is a load of lead;
The moment can only use what the moment itself has bred.

But why do my eyes fasten upon that spot?
Is that little bottle a magnet to my sight?
Why do I feel of a sudden this lovely illumination
As when the moon flows round us in a dark wood at night?

Bottle, unique little bottle, I salute you
As now I devoutly lift you down. In you
I honour human invention and human skill.
You, the quintessence of all sweet narcotics,
The extract of all rare and deadly powers,
I am your master—show me your good will!
I look on you, my sorrow is mitigated,
I hold you and my struggles are abated,
The flood-tide of my spirit ebbs away, away.
The mirroring waters glitter at my feet,
I am escorted forth on the high seas,
Allured towards new shores by a new day.
A fiery chariot floats on nimble wings
Down to me and I feel myself upbuoyed
To blaze a new trail through the upper air
Into new spheres of energy unalloyed.
Oh this high life, this heavenly rapture! Do *you*
Merit this, you, a moment ago a worm?
Merit it? Aye—only turn your back on the sun
Which enchants the earth, turn your back and be firm!
And brace yourself to tear asunder the gates

Which everyone longs to shuffle past if he can;
Now is the time to act and acting prove
That God's height need not lower the merit of Man;
Nor tremble at that dark pit in which our fancy
Condemns itself to torments of its own framing,
But struggle on and upwards to that passage
At the narrow mouth of which all hell is flaming.
Be calm and take this step, though you should fall
Beyond it into nothing—nothing at all.

And you, you loving-cup of shining crystal—
I have not given a thought to you for years—
Down you come now out of your ancient chest!
You glittered at my ancestors' junketings
Enlivening the serious guest
When with you in his hand he proceeded to toast his
    neighbour—
But to-day no neighbour will take you from my hand.
Here is a juice that makes one drunk in a wink;
It fills you full, you cup, with its brown flood.
It was I who made this, I who had it drawn;
So let my whole soul now make my last drink
A high and gala greeting, a toast to the dawn!

(*He raises the cup to his mouth. There is an outburst of bells and choirs*)

CHORUS OF ANGELS:

        Christ is arisen!
        Joy to mortality
        Whom its own fatally
        Earth-bound morality
        Bound in a prison.

FAUST:

    What a deep booming, what a ringing tone
    Pulls back the cup from my lips—and with such power!
    So soon are you announcing, you deep bells,
    Easter Day's first festive hour?
    You choirs, do you raise so soon the solacing hymn
    That once round the night of the grave rang out from the
    As man's new covenant and dower?   [seraphim

CHORUS OF WOMEN:

> With balm and with spices
> 'Twas we laid him out,
> We who tended him,
> Faithful, devout;
> We wound him in linen,
> Made all clean where he lay,
> Alas—to discover
> Christ gone away.

CHORUS OF ANGELS:

> Christ is arisen!
> The loving one! Blest
> After enduring the
> Grievous, the curing, the
> Chastening test.

FAUST:

> You heavenly music, strong as you are kind,
> Why do you search me out in the dust?
> Better ring forth where men have open hearts!
> I hear your message, my faith it is that lags behind;
> And miracle is the favourite child of faith.
> Those spheres whence peals the gospel of forgiving,
> Those are beyond what I can dare,
> And yet, so used am I from childhood to this sound,
> It even now summons me back to living.
> Once I could feel the kiss of heavenly love
> Rain down through the calm and solemn Sabbath air,
> Could find a prophecy in the full-toned bell,
> A spasm of happiness in a prayer.
> An ineffably sweet longing bound me
> To quest at random through field and wood
> Where among countless burning tears
> I felt a world rise up around me.
> This hymn announced the lively games of youth, the lovely
> Freedom of Spring's own festival;
> Now with its childlike feelings memory holds me back
> From the last and gravest step of all.
> But you, sweet songs of heaven, keep sounding forth!
> My tears well up, I belong once more to earth.

CHORUS OF DISCIPLES:

> Now has the Buried One,
> Lowliness ended,
> Living in lordliness,
> Lordly ascended;
> He in the zest of birth
> Near to creating light;
> We on the breast of earth
> Still in frustrating night!
> He left us, his own ones,
> Pining upon this spot,
> Ah, and lamenting,
> Master, thy lot.

CHORUS OF ANGELS:

> Christ is arisen
> From the womb of decay!
> Burst from your prison,
> Rejoice in the day!
> Praising him actively,
> Practising charity,
> Giving alms brotherly,
> Preaching him wanderingly,
> Promising sanctity,
> You have your Master near,
> You have him here!

EASTER HOLIDAY

(Holidaymakers of all kinds come out through the city gate)

FIRST STUDENT:

      Lord, these strapping wenches they go a lick!
      Hurry up, brother, we must give 'em an escort.
      My programme for to-day is a strong ale,
      A pipe of shag and a girl who's got up chic.

FIRST GIRL:

      Look! Will you look at the handsome boys!
      Really and truly it's degrading;
      They could walk out with the best of us
      And they have to run round scullery-maiding!

SECOND STUDENT:

      Hold on, hold on! There are two coming up behind
      With a very pretty taste in dress;
      One of those girls is a neighbour of mine,
      She appeals to me, I must confess.
      You see how quietly they go
      And yet in the end they'll be taking *us* in tow.

BEGGAR (*singing*):

      Good gentlemen and lovely ladies,
      Rosy of cheek and neat of dress,
      Be kind enough to look upon me
      And see and comfort my distress.
      Leave me not here a hopeless busker!
      Only the giver can be gay.
      A day when all the town rejoices,
      Make it for me a harvest day.

FIRST BURGHER:

>I know nothing better on Sundays or on holidays
>Than to have a chat about war and warlike pother
>When far away, in Turkey say,
>The peoples are socking one another.
>One stands at the window, drinks one's half of mild,
>And sees the painted ships glide down the waterways;
>Then in the evening one goes happily home
>And blesses peace and peaceful days.

SECOND BURGHER:

>Yes indeed, neighbour! That is all right with me.
>They can break heads if they like it so
>And churn up everything topsyturvy.
>But at home let us keep the status quo.

OLD WOMAN:

>Eh, but how smart they look! Pretty young things!
>Whoever saw you should adore you!
>But not so haughty! It's all right—
>Tell me your wish and I can get it for you.

FIRST GIRL:

>Come, Agatha! Such witches I avoid
>In public places—it's much wiser really;
>It's true, she helped me on St. Andrew's night
>To see my future sweetheart clearly.

SECOND GIRL:

>Yes, mine she showed me in a crystal,
>A soldier type with dashing chaps behind him;
>I look around, I seek him everywhere
>And yet—and yet I never find him.

SOLDIERS (*singing*):

>>Castles with towering
>>Walls to maintain them,
>>Girls who have suitors
>>But to disdain them,
>>Would I could gain them!

Bold is the venture,
Lordly the pay.

Hark to the trumpets!
They may be crying
Summons to gladness,
Summons to dying.
Life is a storming!
Life is a splendour!
Maidens and castles
Have to surrender.
Bold is the venture,
Lordly the pay;
Later the soldiers
Go marching away.

(*Faust and Wagner are now walking off on the road to the village*)

FAUST:

River and brook are freed from ice
By the lovely enlivening glance of spring
And hope grows green throughout the dale;
Ancient winter, weakening,
Has fallen back on the rugged mountains
And launches thence his Parthian shafts
Which are merely impotent showers of hail
Streaking over the greening mead;
But the sun who tolerates nothing white.
Amidst all this shaping and stirring of seed,
Wants to enliven the world with colour
And, flowers being lacking, in their lieu
Takes colourful crowds to mend the view.
Turn round and look back from this rise
Towards the town. From the gloomy gate
Look, can you see them surging forth—
A harlequin-coloured crowd in fête!
Sunning themselves with one accord
In homage to the risen Lord
For they themselves to-day have risen:
Out of the dismal room in the slum,
Out of each shop and factory prison,

Out of the stuffiness of the garret,
Out of the squash of the narrow streets,
Out of the churches' reverend night—
One and all have been raised to light.
Look, only look, how quickly the gardens
And fields are sprinkled with the throng,
How the river all its length and breadth
Bears so many pleasure-boats along,
And almost sinking from its load
How this last dinghy moves away.
Even on the furthest mountain tracks
Gay rags continue to look gay.
Already I hear the hum of the village,
Here is the plain man's real heaven—
Great and small in a riot of fun;
Here I'm a man—and dare be one.

WAGNER:

Doctor, to take a walk with you
Is a profit and a privilege for me
But I wouldn't lose my way alone round here,
Sworn foe that I am of all vulgarity.
This fiddling, screaming, skittle-playing,
Are sounds I loathe beyond all measure;
They run amuck as if the devil were in them
And call it music, call it pleasure.

(*They have now reached the village*)

OLD PEASANT:

Doctor, it is most good of you
Not to look down on us to-day
And, pillar of learning that you are,
To mill around with folk at play.
So take this most particular jug
Which we have filled for you at the tap,
This is a pledge and I pray aloud
That it quench your thirst and more mayhap:
As many drops as this can give,
So many days extra may you live.

FAUST:

> Thank you for such a reviving beer
> And now—good health to all men here.

> (*The people collect round him*)

OLD PEASANT:

> Of a truth, Doctor, you have done rightly
> To appear on this day when all are glad,
> Seeing how in times past you proved
> Our own good friend when days were bad.
> Many a man stands here alive
> Whom your father found in the grip
> Of a raging fever and tore him thence
> When he put paid to the pestilence.
> You too—you were a youngster then—
> Where any was ill you went your round,
> Right many a corpse left home feet first
> But you came out of it safe and sound,
> From many a gruelling trial—Aye,
> The helper got help from the Helper on high.

CROWD:

> Health to the trusty man. We pray
> He may live to help us many a day.

FAUST:

> Kneel to the One on high, our friend
> Who teaches us helpers, who help can send.

> (*Faust and Wagner leave the crowd and move on*)

WAGNER:

> You great man, how your heart must leap
> To be so honoured by the masses!
> How happy is he who has such talents
> And from them such a crop can reap!
> The father points you out to his boy,
> They all ask questions, run and jostle,
> The fiddles and the dancers pause
> And, as you pass, they stand in rows

And caps go hurtling in the sky;
They almost kneel to you as though
The eucharist were passing by.

FAUST:

Only a few steps more up to that stone!
Here, after our walk, we will take a rest.
Here I have often sat, thoughtful, alone,
Torturing myself with prayer and fast.
Rich in hope and firm in faith,
With tears and sighs to seven times seven
I thought I could end that epidemic
And force the hand of the Lord of Heaven.
But now the crowd's applause sounds to me like derision.
O could you only read in my inmost heart
How little father and son
Merited their great reputation!
My father was a worthy man who worked in the dark,
Who in good faith but on his own wise
Brooded on Nature and her holy circles
With laborious whimsicalities;
Who used to collect the connoisseurs
Into the kitchen and locked inside
Its black walls pour together divers
Ingredients of countless recipes;
Such was our medicine, the patients died
And no one counted the survivors.
And thus we with our hellish powders
Raged more perniciously than the plague
Throughout this district—valley and town.
Myself I have given the poison to thousands;
They drooped away, *I* must live on to sample
The brazen murderers' renown.

WAGNER:

How can you let that weigh so heavily?
Does not a good man do enough
If he works at the art that he has received
Conscientiously and scrupulously?
As a young man you honour your father,
What he can teach, you take with a will;

As a man you widen the range of knowledge
And your son's range may be wider still.

FAUST:

Happy the man who swamped in this sea of Error
Still hopes to struggle up through the watery wall;
What we don't know is exactly what we need
And what we know fulfils no need at all.
But let us not with such sad thoughts
Make this good hour an hour undone!
Look how the cottages on the green
Shine in the glow of the evening sun!
He backs away, gives way, the day is overspent,
He hurries off to foster life elsewhere.
Would I could press on his trail, on his trail for ever—
Alas that I have no wings to raise me into the air!
Then I should see in an everlasting sunset
The quiet world before my feet unfold,
All of its peaks on fire, all of its vales becalmed,
And the silver brook dispersed in streams of gold.
Not the wild peaks with all their chasms
Could interrupt my godlike flight;
Already the bays of the sea that the sun has warmed
Unfurl upon my marvelling sight.
But in the end the sungod seems to sink away,
Yet the new impulse sets me again in motion,
I hasten on to drink his eternal light,
With night behind me and before me day,
Above me heaven and below me ocean.
A beautiful dream—yet the sun leaves me behind.
Alas, it is not so easy for earthly wing
To fly on level terms with the wings of the mind.
Yet born with each of us is the instinct
That struggles upwards and away
When over our heads, lost in the blue,
The lark pours out her vibrant lay;
When over rugged pine-clad ranges
The eagle hangs on outspread wings
And over lake and over plain
We see the homeward-struggling crane.

WAGNER:

I myself have often had moments of fancifulness
But I never experienced yet an urge like this.
Woods and fields need only a quick look
And *I* shall never envy the bird its pinions.
How differently the joys of the mind's dominions
Draw us from page to page, from book to book.
That's what makes winter nights lovely and snug—
The blissful life that warms you through your body—
And, ah, should you unroll a worthwhile manuscript,
You bring all heaven down into your study.

FAUST:

You are only conscious of one impulse. Never
Seek an acquaintance with the other.
Two souls, alas, cohabit in my breast,
A contract one of them desires to sever.
The one like a rough lover clings
To the world with the tentacles of its senses;
The other lifts itself to Elysian Fields
Out of the mist on powerful wings.
Oh, if there be spirits in the air,
Princes that weave their way between heaven and earth,
Come down to me from the golden atmosphere
And carry me off to a new and colourful life.
Aye, if I only had a magic mantle
On which I could fly abroad, a-voyaging,
I would not barter it for the costliest raiment,
Not even for the mantle of a king.

WAGNER:

Do not invoke the notorious host
Deployed in streams upon the wind,
Preparing danger in a thousand forms
From every quarter for mankind.
Thrusting upon you from the North
Come fanged spirits with arrow tongues;
From the lands of morning they come parching
To feed themselves upon your lungs;
The South despatches from the desert
Incendiary hordes against your brain

And the West a swarm which first refreshes,
Then drowns both you and field and plain.
They are glad to listen, adepts at doing harm,
Glad to obey and so throw dust in our eyes;
They make believe that they are sent from heaven
And lisp like angels, telling lies.
But let us move! The world has already gone grey,
The air is beginning to cool and the mist to fall.
It's in the evening one really values home—
But why do you look so astonished, standing there, staring
    that way?
What's there to see in the dusk that's worth the trouble?

FAUST:

    The black dog, do you mark him ranging through corn
        and stubble?

WAGNER:

    I noticed him long ago; he struck me as nothing much.

FAUST:

    Have a good look at the brute. What do you take him for?

WAGNER:

    For a poodle who, as is the way of such,
    Is trailing his master, worrying out the scent.

FAUST:

    But don't you perceive how in wide spirals around us
    He is getting nearer and nearer of set intent?
    And, unless I'm wrong, a running fire
    Eddies behind him in his wake.

WAGNER:

    I can see nothing but a black poodle;
    It must be your eyes have caused this mistake.

FAUST:

    He is casting, it seems to me, fine nooses of magic
    About our feet as a snare.

WAGNER:

> *I* see him leaping round us uncertainly, timidly,
> Finding instead of his master two strangers there.

FAUST:

> The circle narrows; now he is near.

WAGNER:

> Just a dog, you see; no phantoms here.
> He growls and hesitates, grovels on the green
> And wags his tail. Pure dog routine.

FAUST:

> Heel, sir, heel! Come, fellow, come!

WAGNER:

> He is a real poodle noodle.
> Stand still and he'll sit up and beg;
> Speak to him and he's all over you;
> Lose something and he'll fetch it quick,
> He'll jump in the water after your stick.

FAUST:

> I think you're right, I cannot find a trace
> Of a spirit here; it is all a matter of training.

WAGNER:

> If a dog is well brought up, a wise man even
> Can come to be fond of him in such a case.
> Yes, he fully deserves your name upon his collar,
> He whom the students have found so apt a scholar.

FAUST'S STUDY

(He enters with the poodle)

FAUST:

I have forsaken field and meadow
Which night has laid in a deep bed,
Night that wakes our better soul
With a holy and foreboding dread.
Now wild desires are wrapped in sleep
And all the deeds that burn and break,
The love of Man is waking now,
The love of God begins to wake.

Poodle! Quiet! Don't run hither and thither!
Leave my threshold! Why are you snuffling there?
Lie down behind the stove and rest.
Here's a cushion; it's my best.
Out of doors on the mountain paths
You kept us amused by running riot;
But as my protégé at home
You'll only be welcome if you're quiet.

Ah, when in our narrow cell
The lamp once more imparts good cheer,
Then in our bosom—in the heart
That knows itself—then things grow clear.
Reason once more begins to speak
And the blooms of hope once more to spread;
One hankers for the brooks of life,
Ah, and for life's fountain head.

Don't growl, you poodle! That animal sound
Is not in tune with the holy music
By which my soul is girdled round.
We are used to human beings who jeer
At what they do not understand,

Who grouse at the good and the beautiful
Which often causes them much ado;
But must a dog snarl at it too?

But, ah, already, for all my good intentions
I feel contentment ebbing away in my breast.
Why must the stream so soon run dry
And we be left once more athirst?
I have experienced this so often;
Yet this defect has its compensation,
We learn to prize the supernatural
And hanker after revelation,
Which burns most bright and wins assent
Most in the New Testament.
I feel impelled to open the master text
And this once, with true dedication,
Take the sacred original
And make in my mother tongue my own translation.

(*He opens a Bible*)

It is written: In the beginning was the Word.
Here I am stuck at once. Who will help me on?
I am unable to grant the Word such merit,
I must translate it differently
If I am truly illumined by the spirit.
It is written: In the beginning was the Mind.
But why should my pen scour
So quickly ahead? Consider that first line well.
Is it the Mind that effects and creates all things?
It *should* read: In the beginning was the Power.
Yet, even as I am changing what I have writ,
Something warns me not to abide by it.
The spirit prompts me, I see in a flash what I need,
And write: In the beginning was the Deed!

Dog! If we two are to share this room,
Leave off your baying,
Leave off your barking!
I can't have such a fellow staying
Around me causing all this bother.

One of us or the other
Will have to leave the cell.
Well?
I don't really like to eject you so
But the door is open, you may go.

But what? What do I see?
Can this really happen naturally?
Is it a fact or is it a fraud?
My dog is growing so long and broad!
He raises himself mightily,
That is not a dog's anatomy!
What a phantom have I brought to my house!
He already looks like a river horse
With fiery eyes and frightful jaws—
Aha! But I can give you pause!
For such a hybrid out of hell
Solomon's Key is a good spell.

(*Spirits are heard in the passage*)

SPIRITS:

Captured within there is one of us!
Wait without, follow him none of us!
Like a fox in a snare
An old hell-cat's trembling there.
But on the alert!
Fly against and athwart,
To starboard and port,
And he's out with a spurt!
If help you can take him,
Do not forsake him!
For often, to earn it, he
Helped our fraternity.

FAUST:

First, to confront the beast,
Be the Spell of the Four released:
    Salamander shall glow,
    Undine shall coil,
    Sylph shall vanish
    And gnome shall toil.

One without sense
Of the elements,
Of their force
And proper course,
The spirits would never
Own him for master.

> Vanish in flames,
> Salamander!
> Commingle in babble of streams,
> Undine!
> Shine meteor-like and majestic,
> Sylph!
> Bring help domestic,
> Lubber-fiend! Lubber-fiend!
> Step out of him and make an end!

None of the Four
Is the creature's core.
He lies quite quiet and grins at me,
I have not yet worked him injury.
To exercise you
I'll have to chastise you.

> Are you, rapscallion,
> A displaced devil?
> This sign can level
> Each dark battalion;
> Look at this sign!

He swells up already with bristling spine.

> You outcast! Heed it—
> This name! Can you read it?
> The unbegotten one,
> Unpronounceable,
> Poured throughout Paradise,
> Heinously wounded one?

Behind the stove, bound by my spells,
Look, like an elephant it swells,
Filling up all the space and more,
It threatens to melt away in mist.
Down from the ceiling! Down before—!
Down at your master's feet! Desist!
You see, I have not proved a liar;
I can burn you up with holy fire!

Do not await
The triply glowing light!
Do not await
My strongest brand of necromancy!

(*The mist subsides and Mephistopheles comes forward from behind
the stove, dressed like a travelling scholar*)

MEPHISTOPHELES:

What is the noise about? What might the gentleman fancy?

FAUST:

So that is what the poodle had inside him!
A travelling scholar? That casus makes me laugh.

MEPHISTOPHELES:

My compliments to the learned gentleman.
You have put me in a sweat—not half!

FAUST:

What is your name?

MEPHISTOPHELES:

The question strikes me as petty
For one who holds the Word in such low repute,
Who, far withdrawn from all mere surface,
Aims only at the Essential Root.

FAUST:

With you, you gentry, what is essential
The name more often than not supplies,
As is indeed only too patent
When they call you Fly-God, Corrupter, Father of Lies.
All right, who are you then?

MEPHISTOPHELES:

A part of that Power
Which always wills evil, always procures good.

FAUST:

What do you mean by this conundrum?

MEPHISTOPHELES:

> I am the Spirit which always denies.
> And quite rightly; whatever has a beginning
> Deserves to have an undoing;
> It would be better if nothing began at all.
> Thus everything that you call
> Sin, destruction, Evil in short,
> Is my own element, my resort.

FAUST:

> You call yourself a part, yet you stand before me whole?

MEPHISTOPHELES:

> This is the unassuming truth.
> Whereas mankind, that little world of fools,
> Commonly takes itself for a whole—
> I am a part of the Part which in the beginning was all,
> A part of the darkness which gave birth to light,
> To that haughty light which is struggling now to usurp
> The ancient rank and realm of its mother Night,
> And yet has no success, try as it will,
> Being bound and clamped by bodies still.
> It streams from bodies, bodies it beautifies,
> A body clogs it when it would run,
> And so, I hope, it won't be long
> Till, bodies and all, it is undone.

FAUST:

> Ah, now I know your honourable profession!
> You cannot destroy on a large scale,
> So you are trying it on a small.

MEPHISTOPHELES:

> And, candidly, not getting far at all.
> That which stands over against the Nothing,
> The Something, I mean this awkward world,
> For all my endeavours up to date
> I have failed to get it under foot
> With waves, with storms, with earthquakes, fire—
> Sea and land after all stay put.
> And this damned stuff, the brood of beasts and men,

There is no coming to grips with them;
I've already buried heaps of them!
And always new blood, fresh blood, circulates again.
So it goes on, it's enough to drive one crazy.
A thousand embryos extricate themselves
From air, from water and from earth
In wet and dry and hot and cold.
Had I not made a corner in fire
I should find myself without a berth.

FAUST:

So you when faced with the ever stirring,
The creative force, the beneficent,
Counter with your cold devil's fist
Spitefully clenched but impotent.
You curious son of Chaos, why
Not turn your hand to something else?

MEPHISTOPHELES:

We will give it our serious attention—
But more on that subject by and by.
Might I for this time take my leave?

FAUST:

Why you ask I cannot see.
I have already made your acquaintance;
When you feel like it, call on me.
Here is the window, here is the door—
And a chimney too—if it comes to that.

MEPHISTOPHELES:

I must confess; there's a slight impediment
That stops me making my exit pat,
The pentagram upon your threshold—

FAUST:

So the witch's foot is giving you trouble?
Then tell me, since you're worried by that spell,
How did you ever enter, child of Hell?
How was a spirit like you betrayed?

MEPHISTOPHELES:

> You study that sign! It's not well made;
> One of its corners, do you see,
> The outside one's not quite intact.

FAUST:

> A happy accident in fact!
> Which means you're in my custody?
> I did not intend to set a gin.

MEPHISTOPHELES:

> The dog—he noticed nothing, jumping in;
> The case has now turned round about
> And I, the devil, can't get out.

FAUST:

> Then why not leave there by the window?

MEPHISTOPHELES:

> It is a law for devils and phantoms all:
> By the way that we slip in by the same we must take our
>   leave.
> One's free in the first, in the second one's a thrall.

FAUST:

> So Hell itself has its regulations?
> That's excellent; a contract in that case
> Could be made with you, you gentry—and definite?

MEPHISTOPHELES:

> What we promise, you will enjoy with no reservations,
> Nothing will be nipped off from it.
> But all this needs a little explaining
> And will keep till our next heart-to-heart;
> But now I beg and doubly beg you:
> Let me, just for now, depart.

FAUST:

> But wait yet a minute and consent
> To tell me first some news of moment.

MEPHISTOPHELES:

> Let me go now! I'll soon be back
> To be questioned to your heart's content.

FAUST:

> It was not I laid a trap for you,
> You thrust your own head in the noose.
> A devil in the hand's worth two in hell!
> The second time he'll be longer loose.

MEPHISTOPHELES:

> If you so wish it, I'm prepared
> To keep you company and stay;
> Provided that by my arts the time
> Be to your betterment whiled away.

FAUST:

> I am in favour, carry on—
> But let your art be a pleasing one.

MEPHISTOPHELES:

> My friend, your senses will have more
> Gratification in this hour
> Than in a year's monotony.
> What the delicate spirits sing to you
> And the beauties that they bring to you
> Are no empty, idle wizardry.
> You'll have your sense of smell delighted,
> Your palate in due course excited,
> Your feelings rapt enchantingly.
> Preparation? There's no need,
> We are all here. Strike up! Proceed!

> *(The Spirits sing)*

SPIRITS:

> Vanish, you darkling
> Arches above him,
> That a more witching
> Blue and enriching
> Sky may look in!

If only the darkling
Clouds were unravelled!
Small stars are sparkling,
Suns are more gently
Shining within!
Spiritual beauty
Of the children of Heaven
Swaying and bowing
Floats in the air,
Leanings and longings
Follow them there;
And ribbons of raiment
The breezes have caught
Cover the country,
Cover the arbour
Where, drowning in thought,
Lovers exchange their
Pledges for life.
Arbour on arbour!
Creepers run rife!
Grapes in great wreathing
Clusters are poured into
Vats that are seething,
Wines that are foaming
Pour out in rivulets
Rippling and roaming
Through crystalline stones,
Leaving the sight of
The highlands behind them,
Widening to lakes
Amid the delight of
Green-growing foothills.
And the winged creatures
Sipping their ecstasy,
Sunwards they fly,
Fly to discover
The glittering islands
Which bob on the wave-tops
Deceiving the eye.
There we can hear
Huzzaing in chorus,

A landscape of dancers
Extending before us,
All in the open,
Free as the air.
Some of them climbing
Over the peaks,
Some of them swimming
Over the lakes,
Or floating in space—
All towards existence,
All towards the distance
Of stars that will love them,
The blessing of grace.

MEPHISTOPHELES:

He is asleep. That's fine, you airy, dainty youngsters
You have sung him a real cradle song.
For this performance I am in your debt.
You are not yet the man to hold the devil for long.
Play round him with your sweet dream trickeries
And sink him in a sea of untruth!
But to break the spell upon this threshold
What I need now is a rat's tooth.
And I needn't bother to wave a wand,
I can hear one rustling already, he'll soon respond.
The lord of rats, the lord of mice,
Of flies, frogs, bugs and lice,
Commands you to come out of that
And gnaw away this threshold, rat,
While he takes oil and gives it a few—
So there you come hopping? Quick on your cue!
Now get on the job! The obstructing point
Is on the edge and right in front.
One bite more and the work's done.
Now, Faust, till we meet again, dream on!

FAUST: (*waking*)

Am I defrauded then once more?
Does the throng of spirits vanish away like fog
To prove that the devil appeared to me in a dream
But what escaped was only a dog?

(*The same room. Later*)

FAUST:

> Who's knocking? Come in! *Now* who wants to annoy me?

MEPHISTOPHELES (*outside door*):

> It's I.

FAUST:

> Come in!

MEPHISTOPHELES (*outside door*):

> You must say 'Come in' three times.

FAUST:

> Come in then!

MEPHISTOPHELES (*entering*):

> Thank you; you overjoy me.
> We two, I hope, we shall be good friends;
> To chase those megrims of yours away
> I am here like a fine young squire to-day,
> In a suit of scarlet trimmed with gold
> And a little cape of stiff brocade,
> With a cock's feather in my hat
> And at my side a long sharp blade,
> And the most succinct advice I can give
> Is that you dress up just like me,
> So that uninhibited and free
> You may find out what it means to live.

FAUST:

> The pain of earth's constricted life, I fancy,
> Will pierce me still, whatever my attire;
> I am too old for mere amusement,
> Too young to be without desire.
> How can the world dispel my doubt?
> You must do without, you must do without!
> That is the everlasting song
> Which rings in every ear, which rings,
> And which to us our whole life long
> Every hour hoarsely sings.

I wake in the morning only to feel appalled,
My eyes with bitter tears could run
To see the day which in its course
Will not fulfil a wish for me, not one;
The day which whittles away with obstinate carping
All pleasures—even those of anticipation,
Which makes a thousand grimaces to obstruct
My heart when it is stirring in creation.
And again, when night comes down, in anguish
I must stretch out upon my bed
And again no rest is granted me,
For wild dreams fill my mind with dread.
The God who dwells within my bosom
Can make my inmost soul react;
The God who sways my every power
Is powerless with external fact.
And so existence weighs upon my breast
And I long for death and life—life I detest.

MEPHISTOPHELES:

Yet death is never a wholly welcome guest.

FAUST:

O happy is he whom death in the dazzle of victory
Crowns with the bloody laurel in the battling swirl!
Or he whom after the mad and breakneck dance
He comes upon in the arms of a girl!
O to have sunk away, delighted, deleted,
Before the Spirit of the Earth, before his might!

MEPHISTOPHELES:

Yet I know someone who failed to drink
A brown juice on a certain night.

FAUST:

Your hobby is espionage—is it not?

MEPHISTOPHELES:

Oh I'm not omniscient—but I know a lot.

FAUST:

Whereas that tumult in my soul
Was stilled by sweet familiar chimes
Which cozened the child that yet was in me
With echoes of more happy times,
I now curse all things that encompass
The soul with lures and jugglery
And bind it in this dungeon of grief
With trickery and flattery.
Cursed in advance be the high opinion
That serves our spirit for a cloak!
Cursed be the dazzle of appearance
Which bows our senses to its yoke!
Cursed be the lying dreams of glory,
The illusion that our name survives!
Cursed be the flattering things we own,
Servants and ploughs, children and wives!
Cursed be Mammon when with his treasures
He makes us play the adventurous man
Or when for our luxurious pleasures
He duly spreads the soft divan!
A curse on the balsam of the grape!
A curse on the love that rides for a fall!
A curse on hope! A curse on faith!
And a curse on patience most of all!

(*The invisible Spirits sing again*)

SPIRITS:

Woe! Woe!
You have destroyed it,
The beautiful world;
By your violent hand
'Tis downward hurled!
A half-god has dashed it asunder!
From under
We bear off the rubble to nowhere
And ponder
Sadly the beauty departed.
Magnipotent
One among men,
Magnificent

> Build it again,
> Build it again in your breast!
> Let a new course of life
> Begin
> With vision abounding
> And new songs resounding
> To welcome it in!

MEPHISTOPHELES:

> These are the juniors
> Of my faction.
> Hear how precociously they counsel
> Pleasure and action.
> Out and away
> From your lonely day
> Which dries your senses and your juices
> Their melody seduces.
>
> Stop playing with your grief which battens
> Like a vulture on your life, your mind!
> The worst of company would make you feel
> That you are a man among mankind.
> Not that it's really my proposition
> To shove you among the common men;
> Though I'm not one of the Upper Ten,
> If you would like a coalition
> With me for your career through life,
> I am quite ready to fit in,
> I'm yours before you can say knife.
> I am your comrade;
> If you so crave,
> I am your servant, I am your slave.

FAUST:

> And what have I to undertake in return?

MEPHISTOPHELES:

> Oh it's early days to discuss what that is.

FAUST:

> No, no, the devil is an egoist
> And ready to do nothing gratis

Which is to benefit a stranger.
Tell me your terms and don't prevaricate!
A servant like you in the house is a danger.

MEPHISTOPHELES:

I will bind myself to your service in this world,
To be at your beck and never rest nor slack;
When we meet again on the other side,
In the same coin you shall pay me back.

FAUST:

The other side gives me little trouble;
First batter this present world to rubble,
Then the other may rise—if that's the plan.
This earth is where my springs of joy have started,
And this sun shines on me when broken-hearted;
If I can first from them be parted,
Then let happen what will and can!
I wish to hear no more about it—
Whether there too men hate and love
Or whether in those spheres too, in the future,
There is a Below or an Above.

MEPHISTOPHELES:

With such an outlook you can risk it.
Sign on the line! In these next days you will get
Ravishing samples of my arts;
I am giving you what never man saw yet.

FAUST:

Poor devil, can *you* give anything ever?
Was a human spirit in its high endeavour
Even once understood by one of your breed?
Have you got food which fails to feed?
Or red gold which, never at rest,
Like mercury runs away through the hand?
A game at which one never wins?
A girl who, even when on my breast,
Pledges herself to my neighbour with her eyes?
The divine and lovely delight of honour

Which falls like a falling star and dies?
Show me the fruits which, before they are plucked, decay
And the trees which day after day renew their green!

MEPHISTOPHELES:

Such a commission doesn't alarm me,
I have such treasures to purvey.
But, my good friend, the time draws on when we
Should be glad to feast at our ease on something good.

FAUST:

If ever I stretch myself on a bed of ease,
Then I am finished! Is that understood?
If ever your flatteries can coax me
To be pleased with myself, if ever you cast
A spell of pleasure that can hoax me—
Then let *that* day be my last!
That's my wager!

MEPHISTOPHELES:

Done!

FAUST:

Let's shake!
If ever I say to the passing moment
'Linger a while! Thou art so fair!'
Then you may cast me into fetters,
I will gladly perish then and there!
Then you may set the death-bell tolling,
Then from my service you are free,
The clock may stop, its hand may fall,
And that be the end of time for me!

MEPHISTOPHELES:

Think what you're saying, we shall not forget it.

FAUST:

And you are fully within your rights;
I have made no mad or outrageous claim.
If I stay as I am, I am a slave—
Whether yours or another's, it's all the same.

MEPHISTOPHELES:

> I shall this very day at the College Banquet
> Enter your service with no more ado,
> But just one point—As a life-and-death insurance
> I must trouble you for a line or two.

FAUST:

> So you, you pedant, you too like things in writing?
> Have you never known a man? Or a man's word? **Never?**
> Is it not enough that my word of mouth
> Puts all my days in bond for ever?
> Does not the world rage on in all its streams
> And shall a promise hamper *me*?
> Yet this illusion reigns within our hearts
> And from it who would be gladly free?
> Happy the man who can inwardly keep his word;
> Whatever the cost, he will not be loath to pay!
> But a parchment, duly inscribed and sealed,
> Is a bogey from which all wince away.
> The word dies on the tip of the pen
> And wax and leather lord it then.
> What do you, evil spirit, require?
> Bronze, marble, parchment, paper?
> Quill or chisel or pencil of slate?
> You may choose whichever you desire.

MEPHISTOPHELES:

> How can you so exaggerate
> With such a hectic rhetoric?
> Any little snippet is quite good—
> And you sign it with one little drop of blood.

FAUST:

> If that is enough and is some use,
> One may as well pander to your fad.

MEPHISTOPHELES:

> Blood is a very special juice.

FAUST:

> Only do not fear that I shall break this contract.
> What I promise is nothing more

Than what all my powers are striving for.
I have puffed myself up too much, it is only
Your sort that really fits my case.
The great Earth Spirit has despised me
And Nature shuts the door in my face.
The thread of thought is snapped asunder,
I have long loathed knowledge in all its fashions.
In the depths of sensuality
Let us now quench our glowing passions!
And at once make ready every wonder
Of unpenetrated sorcery!
Let us cast ourselves into the torrent of time,
Into the whirl of eventfulness,
Where disappointment and success,
Pleasure and pain may chop and change
As chop and change they will and can;
It is restless action makes the man.

MEPHISTOPHELES:

No limit is fixed for you, no bound;
If you'd like to nibble at everything
Or to seize upon something flying round—
Well, may you have a run for your money!
But seize your chance and don't be funny!

FAUST:

I've told you, it is no question of happiness.
The most painful joy, enamoured hate, enlivening
Disgust—I devote myself to all excess.
My breast, now cured of its appetite for knowledge,
From now is open to all and every smart,
And what is allotted to the whole of mankind
That will I sample in my inmost heart,
Grasping the highest and lowest with my spirit,
Piling men's weal and woe upon my neck,
To extend myself to embrace all human selves
And to founder in the end, like them, a wreck.

MEPHISTOPHELES:

O believe *me*, who have been chewing
These iron rations many a thousand year,

No human being can digest
This stuff, from the cradle to the bier.
This universe—believe a devil—
Was made for no one but a god!
He exists in eternal light
But *us* he has brought into the darkness
While *your* sole portion is day and night.

FAUST:

I will all the same!

MEPHISTOPHELES:

That's very nice.
There's only one thing I find wrong;
Time is short, art is long.
You could do with a little artistic advice.
Confederate with one of the poets
And let him flog his imagination
To heap all virtues on your head,
A head with such a reputation:
Lion's bravery,
Stag's velocity,
Fire of Italy,
Northern tenacity.
Let *him* find out the secret art
Of combining craft with a noble heart
And of being in love like a young man,
Hotly, but working to a plan.
Such a person—*I'd* like to meet him;
'Mr. Microcosm' is how I'd greet him.

FAUST:

What am I then if fate must bar
My efforts to reach that crown of humanity
After which all my senses strive?

MEPHISTOPHELES:

You are in the end . . . what you are.
You can put on full-bottomed wigs with a million locks,
You can put on stilts instead of your socks,
You remain for ever what you are.

FAUST:

> I feel my endeavours have not been worth a pin
> When I raked together the treasures of the human mind,
> If at the end I but sit down to find
> No new force welling up within.
> I have not a hair's breadth more of height,
> I am no nearer the Infinite.

MEPHISTOPHELES:

> My very good sir, you look at things
> Just in the way that people do;
> We must be cleverer than that
> Or the joys of life will escape from you.
> Hell! You have surely hands and feet,
> Also a head and you-know-what;
> The pleasures I gather on the wing,
> Are they less mine? Of course they're not!
> Suppose I can afford six stallions,
> I can add that horse-power to my score
> And dash along and be a proper man
> As if my legs were twenty-four.
> So good-bye to thinking! On your toes!
> The world's before us. Quick! Here goes!
> I tell you, a chap who's intellectual
> Is like a beast on a blasted heath
> Driven in circles by a demon
> While a fine green meadow lies round beneath.

FAUST:

> How do we start?

MEPHISTOPHELES:

> We just say go—and skip.
> But please get ready for this pleasure trip.

> (*Exit Faust*)

> Only look down on knowledge and reason,
> The highest gifts that men can prize,
> Only allow the spirit of lies
> To confirm you in magic and illusion,

And then I have you body and soul.
Fate has given this man a spirit
Which is always pressing onwards, beyond control,
And whose mad striving overleaps
All joys of the earth between pole and pole.
Him shall I drag through the wilds of life
And through the flats of meaninglessness,
I shall make him flounder and gape and stick
And to tease his insatiableness
Hang meat and drink in the air before his watering lips;
In vain he will pray to slake his inner thirst,
And even had he not sold himself to the devil
He would be equally accursed.

(*Re-enter Faust*)

FAUST:

And now, where are we going?

MEPHISTOPHELES:

Wherever you please.
The small world, then the great for us.
With what pleasure and what profit
You will roister through the syllabus!

FAUST:

But I, with this long beard of mine,
I lack the easy social touch,
I know the experiment is doomed;
Out in the world I never could fit in much.
I feel so small in company
I'll be embarrassed constantly.

MEPHISTOPHELES:

My friend, it will solve itself, any such misgiving;
Just trust yourself and you'll learn the art of living.

FAUST:

Well, then, how do we leave home?
Where are your grooms? Your coach and horses?

MEPHISTOPHELES.

> We merely spread this mantle wide,
> It will bear us off on airy courses.
> But do not on this noble voyage
> Cumber yourself with heavy baggage.
> A little inflammable gas which I'll prepare
> Will lift us quickly into the air.
> If we travel light we shall cleave the sky like a knife.
> Congratulations on your new course of life!

THE WITCH'S KITCHEN[1]

(Every sort of witch prop. A large cauldron hangs over the fire. Monkeys sit around it, seen through the fumes)

MEPHISTOPHELES:

    Look, what a pretty species of monkey!
    She is the kitchen-maid, he is the flunkey.
    It seems your mistress isn't at home?

MONKEYS:

        Out at a rout!
        Out and about!
        By the chimney spout!

MEPHISTOPHELES:

    How long does she keep it up at night?

MONKEYS:

    As long as we warm our paws at this fire.

MEPHISTOPHELES:

    How do you like these delicate animals?

FAUST:

    I never saw such an outré sight.
    I find it nauseating, this crazy witchcraft!
    Do you promise me that I shall improve
    In this cesspit of insanity?
    Do I need advice from an old hag?
    And can this filthy brew remove
    Thirty years from my age? O vanity,
    If you know nothing better than this!
    My hope has already vanished away.
    Surely Nature, surely a noble spirit
    Has brought some better balm to the light of day?

[1] Certain transpositions have been made in this scene.

MEPHISTOPHELES:

>My friend, you once more talk to the point.
>There is also a natural means of rejuvenation;
>But that is written in another book
>And is a chapter that needs some explanation.

FAUST:

>I want to know it.

MEPHISTOPHELES:

>Right. There is a means requires
>No money, no physician, and no witch:
>Away with you this moment back to the land,
>And there begin to dig and ditch,
>Confine yourself, confine your mind,
>In a narrow round, ever repeating,
>Let your diet be of the simplest kind,
>Live with the beasts like a beast and do not think it
>>cheating
>To use your own manure to insure your crops are
>>weighty!
>Believe me, that is the best means
>To keep you young till you are eighty.

FAUST:

>I am not used to it, I cannot change
>My nature and take the spade in hand.
>The narrow life is not my style at all.

MEPHISTOPHELES:

>Then it's a job for the witch to arrange.

FAUST:

>The hag—but why do we need just her?
>Can you yourself not brew the drink?

MEPHISTOPHELES:

>A pretty pastime! I'd prefer
>To build a thousand bridges in that time.
>It is not only art and science
>That this work needs but patience too.

A quiet spirit is busy at it for years
And time but fortifies the subtle brew.
And the most wonderful ingredients
Go into it—you couldn't fake it!
The devil taught it her, I admit;
The devil, however, cannot make it.
Tell me, you monkeys, you damned puppets,
What are you doing with that great globe?

He-Monkey:

This is the world:
It rises and falls
And rolls every minute;
It rings like glass—
But how soon it breaks!
And there's nothing in it.
It glitters here
And here still more:
I am alive!
O my son, my dear,
Keep away, keep away!
You are bound to die!
The shards are sharp,
It was made of clay.

(*Faust has meanwhile been gazing in a mirror*)

Faust:

What do I see in this magic mirror?
What a heavenly image to appear!
O Love, lend me the swiftest of your wings
And waft me away into her sphere!
But, alas, when I do not keep this distance,
If to go nearer I but dare
I can see her only as if there were mist in the air—
The fairest image of a woman!
But can Woman be so fair?
In that shape in the mirror must I see the quintessence
Of all the heavens—reclining there?
Can such a thing be found on earth?

MEPHISTOPHELES:

> Naturally, when a God works six days like a black
> And at the end of it slaps himself on the back,
> Something should come of it of some worth.
> For this occasion look your fill.
> I can smell you out a sweetheart as good as this,
> And happy the man who has the luck
> To bear her home to wedded bliss.

> (*The Witch enters down the chimney—violently*)

WITCH:

> What goes on here?
> Who are you two?
> What d'you want here?
> Who has sneaked through?
> May the fever of fire
> Harrow your marrow!

MEPHISTOPHELES:

> Don't you know me, you bag of bones? You monster, you!
> Don't you know your lord and master?
> What prevents me striking you
> And your monkey spirits, smashing you up like plaster?
> Has my red doublet no more claim to fame?
> Can you not recognize the cock's feather?
> Have I concealed my countenance?
> Must I myself announce my name?

WITCH:

> My lord, excuse this rude reception.
> It is only I miss your cloven foot.
> And where is your usual brace of ravens?

MEPHISTOPHELES:

> I'll forgive you this once, as an exception;
> Admittedly some time has pass't
> Since we two saw each other last.
> Culture too, which is licking the whole world level,
> Has latterly even reached the devil.
> The Nordic spook no longer commands a sale;

Where can you see horns, claws or tail?
And as regards the foot, which is my *sine qua non*,
It would prejudice me in the social sphere;
Accordingly, as many young men have done,
I have worn false calves this many a year.

WITCH:

Really and truly I'm knocked flat
To see Lord Satan here again!

MEPHISTOPHELES:

Woman, you must not call me that!

WITCH:

Why! What harm is there in the name?

MEPHISTOPHELES:

Satan has long been a myth without sense or sinew;
Not that it helps humanity all the same,
They are quit of the Evil One but the evil ones continue.
You may call me the Noble Baron, that should do;
I am a cavalier among other cavaliers,
You needn't doubt my blood is blue—

(*He makes an indecent gesture*)

WITCH:

Ha! Ha! Always true to type!
You still have the humour of a guttersnipe!

MEPHISTOPHELES:

Observe my technique, my friend—not a single hitch;
This is the way to get round a witch.

WITCH:

Now tell me, gentlemen, what do you want?

MEPHISTOPHELES:

A good glass of your well-known juice.
And please let us have your oldest vintage;
When it's been kept it's twice the use.

WITCH:

>Delighted! Why, there's some here on the shelf—
>I now and then take a nip myself—
>And, besides, this bottle no longer stinks;
>You're welcome while I've a drop to give.
>*(aside):* But, if this man is unprepared when he drinks,
>You very well know he has not an hour to live.

MEPHISTOPHELES:

>He's a good friend and it should set him up;
>I'd gladly grant him the best of your kitchen,
>So draw your circle and do your witching
>And give the man a decent cup.

>*(The Witch begins her conjuration)*

FAUST:

>But, tell me, how will this mend my status?
>These lunatic gestures, this absurd apparatus,
>This most distasteful conjuring trick—
>I've known it all, it makes me sick.

MEPHISTOPHELES:

>Pooh, that's just fooling, get it in focus,
>And don't be such a prig for goodness' sake!
>As a doctor she must do her hocus-pocus
>So that when you have drunk your medicine it will take.

WITCH:

>The lofty power
>That is wisdom's dower,
>Concealed from great and clever,
>Don't use your brain
>And that's your gain—
>No trouble whatsoever.

FAUST:

>What nonsense is she saying to us?
>My head is splitting; I've the sensation
>Of listening to a hundred thousand
>Idiots giving a mass recitation.

MEPHISTOPHELES:

>Enough, enough, you excellent Sibyl!
>Give us your drink and fill the cup
>Full to the brim and don't delay!
>This draught will do my friend no injury;
>He is a man of more than one degree
>And has drunk plenty in his day.

>*(The Witch gives Faust the cup)*

>Now lower it quickly. Bottoms up!
>And your heart will begin to glow and perk.
>Now out of the circle! You mustn't rest.

WITCH:

>I hope the little drink will work.

MEPHISTOPHELES:

>*(to Witch)* And you, if there's anything you want, all right;
>Just mention it to me on Walpurgis Night.
>*(to Faust)* Come now, follow me instantly!
>You've got to perspire, it's necessary,
>That the drug may pervade you inside and out.
>I can teach you later to value lordly leisure
>And you soon will learn with intensest pleasure
>How Cupid stirs within and bounds about.

FAUST:

>Just one more look, one quick look, in the mirror!
>That woman was too fair to be true.

MEPHISTOPHELES:

>No, no! The paragon of womanhood
>Will soon be revealed in the flesh to you.
>*(aside)* With a drink like this in you, take care—
>You'll soon see Helens everywhere.

IN THE STREET

(Faust accosts Gretchen as she passes)

FAUST:

My pretty young lady, might I venture
To offer you my arm and my escort too?

GRETCHEN:

I'm not a young lady nor am I pretty
And I can get home without help from you.

(She releases herself and goes off)

FAUST:

By Heaven, she's beautiful, this child!
I have never seen her parallel.
So decorous, so virtuous,
And just a little pert as well.
The light of her cheek, her lip so red,
I shall remember till I'm dead!
The way that she cast down her eye
Is stamped on my heart as with a die;
And the way that she got rid of me
Was a most ravishing thing to see!

(Enter Mephistopheles)

Listen to me! Get me that girl!

MEPHISTOPHELES:
Which one?

FAUST:

The one that just went past.

MEPHISTOPHELES:
She? She was coming from her priest,
Absolved from her sins one and all;

I'd crept up near the confessional.
An innocent thing. Innocent? Yes!
At church with nothing to confess!
Over that girl I have no power.

FAUST:

Yet she's fourteen if she's an hour.

MEPHISTOPHELES:

Why, you're talking like Randy Dick
Who covets every lovely flower
And all the favours, all the laurels,
He fancies are for him to pick;
But it doesn't always work out like that.

FAUST:

My dear Professor of Ancient Morals,
Spare me your trite morality!
I tell you straight—and hear me right—
Unless this object of delight
Lies in my arms this very night,
At midnight we part company.

MEPHISTOPHELES:

Haven't you heard: more haste less speed?
A fortnight is the least I need
Even to work up an occasion.

FAUST:

If I had only seven hours clear,
I should not need the devil here
To bring *this* quest to consummation.

MEPHISTOPHELES:

It's almost French, your line of talk;
I only ask you not to worry.
Why make your conquest in a hurry?
The pleasure is less by a long chalk
Than when you first by hook and by crook
Have squeezed your doll and moulded her,

Using all manner of poppycock
That foreign novels keep in stock.

FAUST:

I am keen enough without all that.

MEPHISTOPHELES:

Now, joking apart and without aspersion,
You cannot expect, I tell you flat,
This beautiful child in quick reversion.
Immune to all direct attack—
We must lay our plots behind her back.

FAUST:

Get me something of my angel's!
Carry me to her place of rest!
Get me a garter of my love's!
Get me a kerchief from her breast!

MEPHISTOPHELES:

That you may see the diligent fashion
In which I shall abet your passion,
We won't let a moment waste away,
I will take you to her room to-day.

FAUST:

And shall I see her? Have her?

MEPHISTOPHELES:

No!
She will be visiting a neighbour.
But you in the meanwhile, quite alone,
Can stay in her aura in her room
And feast your fill on joys to come.

FAUST:

Can we go now?

MEPHISTOPHELES:

It is still too soon.

FAUST:

> Then a present for her! Get me one!
>
> *(Exit Faust)*

MEPHISTOPHELES:

> Presents already? Fine. A certain hit!
> I know plenty of pretty places
> And of long-buried jewel-cases;
> I must take stock of them a bit.

GRETCHEN'S ROOM

GRETCHEN (*alone, doing her hair*):
>I'd give a lot to be able to say
>Who the gentleman was to-day.
>He cut a fine figure certainly
>And is sprung from the nobility;
>His face showed that—Besides, you see,
>He'd otherwise not have behaved so forwardly.

(*She goes out; then Mephistopheles and Faust enter*)

MEPHISTOPHELES:
>Come in—very quietly—Only come in!

FAUST (*after a silence*):
>I ask you: please leave me alone!

MEPHISTOPHELES:
>Not all girls keep their room so clean.

FAUST (*looking around*):
>Welcome, sweet gleaming of the gloaming
>That through this sanctuary falls aslope!
>Seize on my heart, sweet fever of love
>That lives and languishes on the dews of hope!
>What a feeling of quiet breathes around me,
>Of order, of contentedness!
>What fulness in this poverty,
>And in this cell what blessedness!
>
>Here I could while away hour after hour.
>It was here, O Nature, that your fleeting **dreams**
>Brought this born angel to full flower.
>Here lay the child and the warm life
>Filled and grew in her gentle breast,

And here the pure and holy threads
Wove a shape of the heavenliest.

And you! What brought you here to-day?
Why do I feel this deep dismay?
What do you want here? Why is your heart so sore?
Unhappy Faust! You are Faust no more.

Is this an enchanted atmosphere?
To have her at once was all my aim,
Yet I feel my will dissolve in a lovesick dream.
Are we the sport of every current of air?

And were she this moment to walk in,
You would pay for this outrage, how you would pay!
The big man, now, alas, so small,
Would lie at her feet melted away.

MEPHISTOPHELES:

Quick! I can see her coming below.

FAUST:

Out, yes out! I'll never come back!

MEPHISTOPHELES:

Here is a casket, it's middling heavy,
I picked it up in a place I know.
Only put it at once here in the cupboard,
I swear she won't believe her eyes;
I put some nice little trinkets in it
In order to win a different prize.
Still child is child and a game's a game.

FAUST:

I don't know; shall I?

MEPHISTOPHELES:

You ask? For shame!
Do you perhaps intend to keep the spoil?
Then I advise Your Lustfulness

To save these hours that are so precious
And save me any further toil.
I hope you aren't avaricious.
After scratching my head so much and twisting my
    hands—

(*He puts the casket in the cupboard*)

Now quick! We depart!
In order to sway the dear young thing
To meet the dearest wish of your heart;
And *you* assume
A look that belongs to the lecture room,
As if Physics and Metaphysics too
Stood grey as life in front of you!
Come on!

(*They go out; then Gretchen reappears*)

GRETCHEN:

It is so sultry, so fusty here,
And it's not even so warm outside.
I feel as if I don't know what—
I wish my mother would appear.
I'm trembling all over from top to toe—
I'm a silly girl to get frightened so.

(*She sings as she undresses*)

There was a king in Thule
Was faithful to the grave,
To whom his dying lady
A golden winecup gave.

He drained it at every banquet—
A treasure none could buy;
Whenever he filled and drank it
The tears o'erflowed his eye.

And when his days were numbered
He numbered land and pelf;
He left his heir his kingdom,
The cup he kept himself.

He sat at the royal table
With his knights of high degree
In the lofty hall of his fathers
In the castle on the sea.

There stood the old man drinking
The last of the living glow,
Then threw the sacred winecup
Into the waves below.

He saw it fall and falter
And founder in the main;
His eyelids fell, thereafter
He never drank again.

(She opens the cupboard to put away her clothes and sees the casket)

How did this lovely casket get in here?
I locked the cupboard, I'm quite sure.
But what can be in it? It's very queer.
Perhaps someone left it here in pawn
And my mother gave him a loan on it.
Here's a little key tied on with tape—
I've a good mind to open it.
What is all this? My God! But see!
I have never come across such things.
Jewels—that would suit a countess
At a really grand festivity.
To whom can these splendid things belong?

(She tries on the jewels and looks in the looking-glass)

If only the ear-rings belonged to me!
They make one look quite differently.
What is the use of looks and youth?
That's all very well and fine in truth
But people leave it all alone,
They praise you and pity you in one;
Gold is their sole
Concern and goal.
Alas for us who have none!

(Elsewhere and later. Mephistopheles joins Faust)

MEPHISTOPHELES:

> By every despised love! By the elements of hell!
> I wish I knew something worse to provide a curse as well!

FAUST:

> What's the trouble? What's biting you?
> I never saw such a face in my life.

MEPHISTOPHELES:

> I would sell myself to the devil this minute
> If only I weren't a devil too.

FAUST:

> What is it? Are you mad? Or sick?
> It suits you to rage like a lunatic!

MEPHISTOPHELES:

> Imagine! The jewels that Gretchen got,
> A priest has gone and scooped the lot!
> Her mother got wind of it and she
> At once had the horrors secretly.
> That woman has a nose beyond compare,
> She's always snuffling in the Book of Prayer,
> And can tell by how each object smells
> If it is sacred or something else;
> So the scent of the jewels tells her clear
> There's nothing very blessed here.
> 'My child,' she cries, 'unrighteous wealth
> Invests the soul, infects the health.
> We'll dedicate it to the Virgin
> And *she'll* make heavenly manna burgeon!'
> Gretchen's face, you could see it fall;
> She thought: 'It's a gift-horse after all,
> And he *can't* be lacking in sanctity
> Who brought it here so handsomely!'
> The mother had a priest along
> And had hardly started up her song
> Before he thought things looked all right
> And said: 'Very proper and above board!
> Self-control is its own reward.

The Church has an excellent appetite,
She has swallowed whole countries and the question
Has never arisen of indigestion.
Only the Church, my dears, can take
Ill-gotten goods without stomach-ache!'

FAUST:

That is a custom the world through,
A Jew and a king observe it too.

MEPHISTOPHELES:

So brooch, ring, chain he swipes at speed
As if they were merely chicken-feed,
Thanks them no more and no less for the casket
Than for a pound of nuts in a basket,
Promises Heaven will provide
And leaves them extremely edified.

FAUST:

And Gretchen?

MEPHISTOPHELES:

Sits and worries there,
Doesn't know what to do and doesn't care,
Thinks day and night on gold and gem,
Still more on the man who presented them.

FAUST:

My sweetheart's grief distresses me.
Get her more jewels instantly!
The first lot barely deserved the name.

MEPHISTOPHELES:

So the gentleman thinks it all a nursery game!

FAUST:

Do what I tell you and get it right;
Don't let her neighbour out of your sight.
And don't be a sloppy devil; contrive
A new set of jewels. Look alive!

(Exit Faust)

MEPHISTOPHELES:
>Yes, my dear sir, with all my heart.
>This is the way that a fool in love
>Puffs away to amuse his lady
>Sun and moon and the stars above.

MARTHA'S HOUSE

MARTHA (*alone*):

> My dear husband, God forgive him,
> His behaviour has *not* been without a flaw!
> Careers away out into the world
> And leaves me alone to sleep on straw.
> And yet I never trod on his toes,
> I loved him with all my heart, God knows. (*Sobs*)
> Perhaps he is even dead—O fate!
> If I'd only a death certificate!

(*Gretchen enters*)

GRETCHEN:

> Frau Martha!

MARTHA:

> Gretelchen! What's up?

GRETCHEN:

> My legs are sinking under me,
> I've just discovered in my cupboard
> Another casket—of ebony,
> And things inside it, such a store,
> Far richer than the lot before.

MARTHA:

> You mustn't mention it to your mother;
> She'd take it straight to the priest—like the other.

GRETCHEN:

> But only look! Just look at this!

MARTHA:

> O you lucky little Miss!

GRETCHEN:

I daren't appear in the street, I'm afraid,
Or in church either, thus arrayed.

MARTHA:

Just you visit me often here
And put on the jewels secretly!
Walk up and down for an hour in front of my glass
And that will be fun for you and me;
And then an occasion may offer, a holiday,
Where one can let them be seen in a gradual way;
A necklace to start with, then a pearl ear-ring; your
    mother
Most likely won't see; if she does one can think up some-
    thing or other.

GRETCHEN:

But who brought these two cases, who could it be?
It doesn't seem quite right to me.

(Knocking)

My God! My mother? Is that her?

MARTHA:

It is a stranger. Come in, sir!

(Enter Mephistopheles)

MEPHISTOPHELES:

I have made so free as to walk straight in;
The ladies will pardon me? May I begin
By inquiring for a Frau Martha Schwerdtlein?

MARTHA:

That's me. What might the gentleman want?

MEPHISTOPHELES (*aside to Martha*):

Now I know who you are, that's enough for me;
You have very distinguished company.
Forgive my bursting in so soon;
I will call again in the afternoon.

MARTHA:

> Imagine, child, in the name of Piety!
> The gentleman takes you for society.

GRETCHEN:

> I'm a poor young thing, not at all refined;
> My God, the gentleman is too kind.
> These jewels and ornaments aren't my own.

MEPHISTOPHELES:

> Oh, it's not the jewellery alone;
> She has a presence, a look so keen—
> How delighted I am that I may remain.

MARTHA:

> What is your news? I cannot wait—

MEPHISTOPHELES:

> I wish I'd a better tale to relate.
> I trust this will not earn me a beating:
> Your husband is dead and sends his greeting.

MARTHA:

> Dead? The good soul? Oh why! Oh why!
> My husband is dead! Oh I shall die!

GRETCHEN:

> Oh don't, dear woman, despair so.

MEPHISTOPHELES:

> Listen to my tale of woe!

GRETCHEN:

> Now, while I live, may I never love;
> Such a loss would bring me to my grave.

MEPHISTOPHELES:

> Joy must have grief, grief must have joy.

MARTHA:

> How was his end? Oh tell it me.

MEPHISTOPHELES:

> He lies buried in Padua
> At the church of Holy Anthony,
> In properly consecrated ground
> Where he sleeps for ever cool and sound.

MARTHA:

> Have you nothing else for me? Is that all?

MEPHISTOPHELES:

> Yes, a request; it's heavy and fat.
> You must have three hundred masses said for his soul.
> My pockets are empty apart from that.

MARTHA:

> What! Not a trinket? Not a token?
> What every prentice keeps at the bottom of his bag
> And saves it up as a souvenir
> And would sooner starve and sooner beg—

MEPHISTOPHELES:

> Madam, you make me quite heart-broken.
> But, really and truly, he didn't squander his money.
> And, besides, he repented his mistakes,
> Yes, and lamented still more his unlucky breaks.

GRETCHEN:

> Alas that men should be so unlucky!
> Be assured I shall often pray that he may find rest above.

MEPHISTOPHELES:

> *You* deserve to be taken straight to the altar;
> You are a child a man could love.

GRETCHEN:

> No, no, it's not yet time for that.

MEPHISTOPHELES:

> Then, if not a husband, a lover will do.
> It's one of the greatest gifts of Heaven
> To hold in one's arms a thing like you.

GRETCHEN:

> That is not the custom of our race.

MEPHISTOPHELES:

> Custom or not, it's what takes place.

MARTHA:

> But tell me!

MEPHISTOPHELES:

> His deathbed, where I stood,
> Was something better than a dungheap—
> Half-rotten straw; however, he died like a Christian
> And found he had still a great many debts to make good
> How thoroughly, he cried, I must hate myself
> To leave my job and my wife like that on the shelf!
> When I remember it, I die!
> If only she would forgive me here below!

MARTHA:

> Good man! I have forgiven him long ago.

MEPHISTOPHELES:

> All the same, God knows, she was more at fault than I.

MARTHA:

> That's a lie! To think he lied at the point of death!

MEPHISTOPHELES:

> He certainly fibbed a bit with his last breath,
> If I'm half a judge of the situation.
> I had no need, said he, to gape for recreation;
> First getting children, then getting bread to feed 'em—
> And bread in the widest sense, you know—
> And I couldn't even eat my share in peace.

MARTHA:

> So all my love, my loyalty, went for naught,
> My toiling and moiling without cease!

MEPHISTOPHELES:

>Not at all; he gave it profoundest thought.
>When I left Malta—that was how he began—
>I prayed for my wife and children like one demented
>And Heaven heard me and consented
>To let us capture a Turkish merchantman,
>With a treasure for the Sultan himself on board.
>Well, bravery got its due reward
>And I myself, as was only fit,
>I got a decent cut of it.

MARTHA:

>Eh! Eh! How? Where? Has he perhaps buried it?

MEPHISTOPHELES:

>Who knows where the four winds now have carried it?
>As he lounged round Naples, quite unknown,
>A pretty lady made him her friend,
>She was so fond of him, so devoted,
>He wore her colours at his blessed end.

MARTHA:

>The crook! The robber of his children!
>Could no misery, no poverty,
>Check the scandalous life he led!

MEPHISTOPHELES:

>You see! That is just why he's dead.
>However, if I were placed like you,
>I would mourn him modestly for a year
>While looking round for someone new.

MARTHA:

>Ah God! My first one was so dear,
>His like in this world will be hard to discover.
>There could hardly be a more sweet little fool than mine.
>It was only he was too fond of playing the rover,
>And of foreign women and foreign wine,
>And of the God-damned gaming-table.

MEPHISTOPHELES:

> Now, now, he might have still got by
> If he on his part had been able
> To follow your suit and wink an eye.
> With that proviso, I swear, I too
> Would give an engagement ring to you.

MARTHA:

> The gentleman is pleased to be witty.

MEPHISTOPHELES (*aside*):

> I had better go while the going's good;
> She'd hold the devil to his word, she would!
> And how is it with *your* heart, my pretty?

GRETCHEN:

> What does the gentleman mean?

MEPHISTOPHELES (*aside*):

> Good, innocent child!
> Farewell, ladies!

GRETCHEN:

> Farewell!

MARTHA:

> O quickly! Tell me;
> I'd like to have the evidence filed
> Where, how and when my treasure died and was buried.
> I have always liked things orderly and decent
> And to read of his death in the weeklies would be
> pleasant.

MEPHISTOPHELES:

> Yes, Madam, when two witnesses are agreed,
> The truth, as we all know, is guaranteed;
> And I have a friend, an excellent sort,
> I'll get him to swear you this in court.
> I'll bring him here.

MARTHA:

O yes! Please do!

MEPHISTOPHELES:

And the young lady will be here too?
He's an honest lad. He's been around,
His politeness to ladies is profound.

GRETCHEN:

I'll be all blushes in his presence.

MEPHISTOPHELES:

No king on earth should so affect you.

MARTHA:

Behind the house there—in my garden—
This evening—both of you—we'll expect you.

IN THE STREET

FAUST:

How is it? Going ahead? Will it soon come right?

MEPHISTOPHELES:

Excellent! Do I find you all on fire?
Gretchen is yours before many days expire.
You will see her at Martha's, her neighbour's house to-night
And that's a woman with a special vocation,
As it were, for the bawd-cum-gipsy occupation.

FAUST:

Good!

MEPHISTOPHELES:

But there is something *we* must do.

FAUST:

One good turn deserves another. True.

MEPHISTOPHELES:

It only means the legal attesting
That her husband's played-out limbs are resting
At Padua in consecrated ground.

FAUST:

Very smart! I suppose we begin by going to Padua!

MEPHISTOPHELES:

There's no need for that. What a simple lad you are!
Only bear witness and don't ask questions.

FAUST:

The scheme's at an end if you have no better suggestions.

MEPHISTOPHELES:

> Oh there you go! What sanctity!
> Is this the first time in your life
> You have committed perjury?
> God and the world and all that moves therein,
> Man and the way his emotions and thoughts take place,
> Have you not given downright definitions
> Of these with an iron breast and a brazen face?
> And if you will only look below the surface,
> You must confess you knew as much of these
> As you know to-day of Herr Schwerdtlein's late decease.

FAUST:

> You are and remain a sophist and a liar.

MEPHISTOPHELES:

> Quite so—if that is as deep as you'll inquire.
> Won't you to-morrow on your honour
> Befool poor Gretchen and swear before her
> That all your soul is set upon her?

FAUST:

> And from my heart.

MEPHISTOPHELES:

> That's nice of you!
> And your talk of eternal faith and love,
> Of one single passion enthroned above
> All others—will that be heartfelt too?

FAUST:

> Stop! It will! If I have feeling, if I
> Feel this emotion, this commotion,
> And can find no name to call it by;
> If then I sweep the world with all my senses casting
> Around for words and all the highest titles
> And call this flame which burns my vitals
> Endless, everlasting, everlasting,
> Is that a devilish game of lies?

MEPHISTOPHELES:

> I'm right all the same.

FAUST:

> Listen! Mark this well,
> I beg you, and spare me talking till I'm hoarse:
> The man who *will* be right, provided he has a tongue,
> Why, he'll be right of course.
> But come, I'm tired of listening to your voice;
> You're right, the more so since I have no choice.

MARTHA'S GARDEN

(They are walking in pairs: Martha with Mephistopheles, Gretchen on Faust's arm)

GRETCHEN:

> The gentleman's only indulging me, I feel,
> And condescending, to put me to shame.
> You travellers are all the same,
> You put up with things out of sheer good will.
> I know too well that my poor conversation
> Can't entertain a person of your station.

FAUST:

> One glance from you, one word, entertains me more
> Than all this world's wisdom and lore

(He kisses her hand)

GRETCHEN:

> Don't go to such inconvenience! How could you kiss my
>   hand?
> It is so ugly, it is so rough.
> I have had to work at Heaven knows what!
> My mother's exacting, true enough.

(They pass on)

MARTHA:

> And you, sir, do you always move round like this?

MEPHISTOPHELES:

> Oh, business and duty keep us up to the minute!
> With what regret one often leaves a place
> And yet one cannot ever linger in it.

MARTHA:

> That may go in one's salad days—

To rush all over the world at random;
But the evil time comes on apace
And to drag oneself to the grave a lonely bachelor
Is never much good in any case.

MEPHISTOPHELES:

The prospect alarms me at a distant glance.

MARTHA:

Then, worthy sir, be wise while you have the chance.

(They pass on)

GRETCHEN:

Yes, out of sight, out of mind!
You are polite to your finger-ends
But you have lots of clever friends
Who must leave *me* so far behind.

FAUST:

Believe me, dearest, what the world calls clever
More often is vanity and narrowness.

GRETCHEN:

What?

FAUST:

Alas that simplicity, that innocence,
Cannot assess itself and its sacred value ever!
That humility, lowliness, the highest gifts
That living Nature has shared out to men—

GRETCHEN:

Only think of *me* one little minute,
I shall have time enough to think of you again.

FAUST:

You are much alone, I suppose?

GRETCHEN:

Yes, our household's only small
But it needs running after all.

We have no maid; I must cook and sweep and knit
And sew and be always on the run,
And my mother looks into every detail—
Each single one.
Not that she has such need to keep expenses down;
We could spread ourselves more than some others do;
My father left us a decent property,
A little house with a garden outside town.
However, my days at the present are pretty quiet;
My brother's in the army,
My little sister is dead.
The child indeed had worn me to a thread;
Still, all that trouble, I'd have it again, I'd try it,
I loved her so.

FAUST:

An angel, if she was like you!

GRETCHEN:

I brought her up, she was very fond of me.
She was born after my father died.
We gave my mother up for lost,
Her life was at such a low, low tide,
And she only got better slowly, bit by bit;
The poor little creature, she could not even
Think for a minute of suckling it;
And so I brought her up quite alone
On milk and water; so she became my own.
On my own arm, on my own knee,
She smiled and kicked, grew fair to see.

FAUST:

You felt, I am sure, the purest happiness.

GRETCHEN:

Yes; and—be sure—many an hour of distress.
The little one's cradle stood at night
Beside my bed; she could hardly stir
But I was awake,
Now having to give her milk, now into my bed with her,

Now, if she went on crying, try to stop her
By getting up and dandling her up and down the room,
And then first thing in the morning stand at the copper;
Then off to the market and attend to the range,
And so on day after day, never a change.
Living like that, one can't always feel one's best;
But food tastes better for it, so does rest.

(They pass on)

MARTHA:

No, the poor women don't come out of it well,
A *vieux garçon* is a hard nut to crack.

MEPHISTOPHELES:

It only rests with you and your like
To put me on a better tack.

MARTHA:

Tell me, sir: have you never met someone you fancy?
Has your heart been nowhere involved among the girls?

MEPHISTOPHELES:

The proverb says: A man's own fireside
And a good wife are gold and pearls.

MARTHA:

I mean, have you never felt any inclination?

MEPHISTOPHELES:

I've generally been received with all consideration.

MARTHA:

What I wanted to say: has your heart never been serious?

MEPHISTOPHELES:

To make a joke to a woman is always precarious.

MARTHA:

Oh you don't understand me!

MEPHISTOPHELES:

> Now *that* I really mind!
> But I do understand—that you are very kind.

> (*They pass on*)

FAUST:

> You knew me again, you little angel,
> As soon as you saw me enter the garden?

GRETCHEN:

> Didn't you see me cast down my eyes?

FAUST:

> And the liberty that I took you pardon?
> The impudence that reared its head
> When you lately left the cathedral door.

GRETCHEN:

> I was upset; it had never happened before;
> No one could ever say anything bad of me—
> Oh can he, I thought, have seen in my behaviour
> Any cheekiness, any impropriety?
> The idea, it seemed, had come to you pat:
> 'I can treat this woman just like that'.
> I must admit I did not know what it was
> In my heart that began to make me change my view,
> But indeed I was angry with myself because
> I could not be angrier with you.

FAUST:

> Sweet love!

GRETCHEN:

> Wait a moment!

> (*She plucks a flower and starts picking off the petals*)

FAUST:

> What is that? A bouquet?

GRETCHEN:

> No, only a game.

FAUST:

> A what?

GRETCHEN:

> You will laugh at me. Go away!

(Gretchen murmurs)

FAUST:

What are you murmuring?

GRETCHEN:

> Loves me—Loves me not—

FAUST:

You flower from Heaven's garden plot!

GRETCHEN:

Loves me—Not—Loves me—Not—
Loves me!

FAUST:

> Yes, child. What this flower has told you
> Regard it as God's oracle. He loves you!
> Do you know the meaning of that? He loves you!

(He takes her hands)

GRETCHEN:

Oh I feel so strange.

FAUST:

> Don't shudder. Let this look,
> Let this clasp of the hand tell you
> What mouth can never express:
> To give oneself up utterly and feel
> A rapture which must be everlasting.
> Everlasting! Its end would be despair.
> No; no end! No end!

*(She breaks away from him and runs off. After a moment's thought
he follows her)*

MARTHA (*approaching*):
>   The night's coming on.

MEPHISTOPHELES:
>   Yes—and we must go.

MARTHA:
>   I would ask you to remain here longer
>   But this is a terrible place, you know.
>   It's as if no one were able to shape at
>   Any vocation or recreation
>   But must have his neighbour's comings and goings to gape
>   at
>   And, whatever one does, the talk is unleashed, unfurled.
>   And our little couple?

MEPHISTOPHELES:
>   Carefree birds of summer!
>   Flown to the summerhouse.

MARTHA:
>   He seems to like her.

MEPHISTOPHELES:
>   And vice versa. That is the way of the world.

A SUMMERHOUSE

(Gretchen runs in and hides behind the door)

GRETCHEN:
>He comes!

FAUST *(entering)*:
>>You rogue! Teasing me so!
>I've caught you!

>>*(He kisses her)*

GRETCHEN:
>>Dearest! I love you so!

>>*(Mephistopheles knocks)*

FAUST:
>Who's there?

MEPHISTOPHELES:
>>A friend.

FAUST:
>>A brute!

MEPHISTOPHELES:
>>>It is time to part, you know.

MARTHA *(joining them)*:
>Yes, it is late, sir.

FAUST:
>>May I not see you home?

GRETCHEN:
>My mother would—Farewell!

FAUST:

                I must go then?
    Farewell!

MARTHA:

              Adieu!

GRETCHEN:

                  Let us soon meet again!

(Faust and Mephistopheles leave)

Dear God! A man of such a kind,
What things must go on in his mind!
I can only blush when he talks to me;
Whatever he says, I must agree.
Poor silly child, I cannot see
What it is he finds in me.

FOREST AND CAVERN

FAUST (*alone*):

    Exalted Spirit, you gave me, gave me all
I prayed for. Aye, and it is not in vain
That you have turned your face in fire upon me.
You gave me glorious Nature for my kingdom
With power to feel her and enjoy her. Nor
Is it a mere cold wondering glance you grant me
But you allow me to gaze into her depths
Even as into the bosom of a friend.
Aye, you parade the ranks of living things
Before me and you teach me to know my brothers
In the quiet copse, in the water, in the air.
And when the storm growls and snarls in the forest
And the giant pine falls headlong, bearing away
And crushing its neighbours, bough and bole and all,
With whose dull fall the hollow hill resounds,
Then do you carry me off to a sheltered cave
And show me myself, and wonders of my own breast
Unveil themselves in their deep mystery.
And now that the clear moon rises on my eyes
To soften things, now floating up before me
From walls of rock and from the dripping covert
Come silver forms of the past which soothe and temper
The dour delight I find in contemplation.

    That nothing perfect falls to men, oh now
I feel that true. In addition to the rapture
Which brings me near and nearer to the gods
You gave me that companion whom already
I cannot do without, though cold and brazen
He lowers me in my own eyes and with
One whispered word can turn your gifts to nothing.
He is always busily fanning in my breast
A fire of longing for that lovely image.

So do I stagger from desire to enjoyment
And in enjoyment languish for desire.

(*Mephistopheles enters*)

MEPHISTOPHELES:

Haven't you yet had enough of this kind of life?
How can it still appeal to you?
It is all very well to try it once,
Then one should switch to something new.

FAUST:

I wish you had something else to do
On my better days than come plaguing me.

MEPHISTOPHELES:

Now, now! I'd gladly leave you alone;
You needn't suggest it seriously.
So rude and farouche and mad a friend
Would certainly be little loss.
One has one's hands full without end!
One can never read in the gentleman's face
What he likes or what should be left alone.

FAUST:

That is exactly the right tone!
He must be thanked for causing me ennui.

MEPHISTOPHELES:

Poor son of earth, what sort of life
Would you have led were it not for me?
The flim-flams of imagination,
I have cured you of those for many a day.
But for me, this terrestrial ball
Would already have seen you flounce away.
Why behave as an owl behaves
Moping in rocky clefts and caves?
Why do you nourish yourself like a toad that sips
From moss that oozes, stone that drips?
A pretty pastime to contrive!
The doctor in you is still alive.

FAUST:

> Do you comprehend what a new and vital power
> This wandering in the wilderness has given me?
> Aye, with even an inkling of such joy,
> You would be devil enough to grudge it me.

MEPHISTOPHELES:

> A supernatural gratification!
> To lie on the mountain tops in the dark and dew
> Rapturously embracing earth and heaven,
> Swelling yourself to a godhead, ferreting through
> The marrow of the earth with divination,
> To feel in your breast the whole six days of creation,
> To enjoy I know not what in arrogant might
> And then, with the Old Adam discarded quite,
> To overflow into all things in ecstasy;
> After all which your lofty intuition

> (*He makes a gesture*)

> Will end—hm—unmentionably.

FAUST:

> Shame on you!

MEPHISTOPHELES:

> Am I to blame?
> *You* have the right to be moral and cry shame!
> One must not mention to the modest ear
> What the modest heart is ever agog to hear.
> And, in a word, you are welcome to the pleasure
> Of lying to yourself in measure;
> But this deception will not last.
> Already overdriven again,
> If this goes on you must collapse,
> Mad or tormented or aghast.
> Enough of this! Back there your love is sitting
> And all her world seems sad and small;
> You are never absent from her mind,
> Her love for you is more than all.
> At first your passion came overflowing
> Like a brook that the melted snows have bolstered high;

You have poured your passion into her heart
And now your brook once more is dry.
I think, instead of lording it here above
In the woods, the great man might think fit
In view of that poor ninny's love
To make her some return for it.
She finds the time wretchedly long;
She stands at the window, watches the clouds
As over the old town walls they roll away.
'If I had the wings of a dove'—so runs her song
Half the night and all the day.
Now she is cheerful, mostly low,
Now has spent all her tears,
Now calm again, it appears,
But always loves you so.

FAUST:

You snake! You snake!

MEPHISTOPHELES (*aside*):
Ha! It begins to take!

FAUST:

You outcast! Take yourself away
And do not name that lovely woman.
Do not bring back the desire for her sweet body
Upon my senses that are half astray.

MEPHISTOPHELES:
Where's this to end? She thinks you have run off,
And so you have—about half and half.

FAUST:

I am still near her and, though far removed,
Her image must be always in my head;
I already envy the body of the Lord
When her lips rest upon the holy bread.

MEPHISTOPHELES:

> Very well, my friend. I have often envied you
> Those two young roes that are twins, I mean her two—

FAUST:

> Pimp! Get away!

MEPHISTOPHELES:

> Fine! So you scold? I must laugh.
> The God who created girl and boy
> Knew very well the high vocation
> Which facilitates their joy.
> But come, this is a fine excuse for gloom!
> You should take the road to your sweetheart's room,
> Rather than that to death, you know.

FAUST:

> What is the joy of heaven in her arms?
> Even when I catch fire upon her breast
> Do I not always sense her woe?
> Am I not the runaway? The man without a home?
> The monster restless and purposeless
> Who roared like a waterfall from rock to rock in foam
> Greedily raging towards the precipice?
> And she on the bank in childlike innocence
> In a little hut on the little alpine plot
> And all her little household world
> Concentrated in that spot.
> And I, the loathed of God,
> I was not satisfied
> To seize and crush to powder
> The rocks on the river side!
> Her too, her peace, I must undermine as well!
> This was the sacrifice I owed to Hell!
> Help, Devil, to shorten my time of torment!
> What must be, must be; hasten it!
> Let her fate hurtle down with mine,
> Let us go together to the pit!

MEPHISTOPHELES:

> How it glows again, how it boils again!
> Go in and comfort her, my foolish friend!
> When such a blockhead sees no outlet
> He thinks at once it is the end.
> Long live the man who does not flinch!
> But you've a devil in you, somewhere there.
> I know of nothing on earth more unattractive
> Than your devil who feels despair.

GRETCHEN'S ROOM

(Gretchen is alone, singing at the spinning-wheel)

GRETCHEN:

My peace is gone,
My heart is sore,
I shall find it never
And never more.

He has left my room
An empty tomb,
He has gone and all
My world is gall.

My poor head
Is all astray,
My poor mind
Fallen away.

My peace is gone,
My heart is sore,
I shall find it never
And never more.

'Tis he that I look through
The window to see,
He that I open
The door for—he!

His gait, his figure,
So grand, so high!
The smile of his mouth,
The power of his eye,

And the magic stream
Of his words—what bliss!
The clasp of his hand
And, ah, his kiss!

My peace is gone,
My heart is sore,
I shall find it never
And never more.

My heart's desire
Is so strong, so vast;
Ah, could I seize him
And hold him fast

And kiss him for ever
Night and day—
And on his kisses
Pass away!

MARTHA'S GARDEN

GRETCHEN:

Promise me, Heinrich!

FAUST:

If I can!

GRETCHEN:

Tell me: how do you stand in regard to religion?
You are indeed a good, good man
But I think you give it scant attention.

FAUST:

Leave that, my child! You feel what I feel for you;
For those I love I would give my life and none
Will I deprive of his sentiments and his church.

GRETCHEN:

That is not right; one must believe thereon.

FAUST:

Must one?

GRETCHEN:

If only I had some influence!
Nor do you honour the holy sacraments.

FAUST:

I honour them.

GRETCHEN:

Yes, but not with any zest.
When were you last at mass, when were you last confessed?
Do you believe in God?

FAUST:

> My darling, who dare say:
> I believe in God?
> Ask professor or priest,
> Their answers will make an odd
> Mockery of you.

GRETCHEN:

> You don't believe, you mean?

FAUST:

> Do not misunderstand me, my love, my queen!
> Who can name him?
> Admit on the spot:
> I believe in him?
> And who can dare
> To perceive and declare:
> I believe in him not?
> The All-Embracing One,
> All-Upholding One,
> Does he not embrace, uphold,
> You, me, Himself?
> Does not the Heaven vault itself above us?
> Is not the earth established fast below?
> And with their friendly glances do not
> Eternal stars rise over us?
> Do not my eyes look into yours,
> And all things thrust
> Into your head, into your heart,
> And weave in everlasting mystery
> Invisibly, visibly, around you?
> Fill your heart with *this*, great as it is,
> And when this feeling grants you perfect bliss,
> Then call it what you will—
> Happiness! Heart! Love! God!
> I have no name for it!
> Feeling is all;
> Name is mere sound and reek
> Clouding Heaven's light.

GRETCHEN:

> That sounds quite good and right;
> And much as the priest might speak,
> Only not word for word.

FAUST:

> It is what all hearts have heard
> In all the places heavenly day can reach,
> Each in his own speech;
> Why not I in mine?

GRETCHEN:

> I could almost accept it, you make it sound so fine,
> Still there is something in it that shouldn't be;
> For you have no Christianity.

FAUST:

> Dear child!

GRETCHEN:

> It has long been a grief to me
> To see you in such company.

FAUST:

> You mean?

GRETCHEN:

> The man who goes about with you,
> I hate him in my soul, right through and through.
> And nothing has given my heart
> In my whole life so keen a smart
> As that man's face, so dire, so grim.

FAUST:

> Dear poppet, don't be afraid of him!

GRETCHEN:

> My blood is troubled by his presence.
> All other people, I wish them well;
> But much as I may long to see you,

He gives me a horror I cannot tell,
And I think he's a man too none can trust.
God forgive me if I'm unjust.

FAUST:

Such queer fish too must have room to swim.

GRETCHEN:

I wouldn't live with the like of him!
Whenever that man comes to the door,
He looks in so sarcastically,
Half angrily,
One can see he feels no sympathy;
It is written on his face so clear
There is not a soul he can hold dear.
I feel so cosy in your arms,
So warm and free from all restraint,
And his presence ties me up inside.

FAUST:

You angel, with your wild alarms!

GRETCHEN:

It makes me feel so ill, so faint,
That, if he merely happens to join us,
I even think I have no more love for you.
Besides, when he's there, I could never pray,
And that is eating my heart away;
You, Heinrich, you must feel it too.

FAUST:

You suffer from an antipathy.

GRETCHEN:

Now I must go.

FAUST:

Oh, can I never rest
One little hour hanging upon your breast,
Pressing both breast on breast and soul on soul?

GRETCHEN:

    Ah, if I only slept alone!
    I'd gladly leave the door unlatched for you to-night;
    My mother, however, sleeps so light
    And if she found us there, I own
    I should fall dead upon the spot.

FAUST:

    You angel, there is no fear of that.
    Here's a little flask. Three drops are all
    It needs—in her drink—to cover nature
    In a deep sleep, a gentle pall.

GRETCHEN:

    What would I not do for your sake!
    I hope it will do her no injury.

FAUST:

    My love, do you think that of me?

GRETCHEN:

    Dearest, I've only to look at you
    And I do not know what drives me to meet your will
    I have already done so much for you
    That little more is left me to fulfil.

        (She goes out—and Mephistopheles enters)

MEPHISTOPHELES:

    The monkey! Is she gone?

FAUST:

          Have you been spying again?

MEPHISTOPHELES:

    I have taken pretty good note of it,
    The doctor has been catechised—
    And much, I hope, to his benefit;
    The girls are really keen to be advised
    If a man belongs to the old simple-and-pious school.
    'If he stand that', they think, 'he'll stand *our* rule.'

FAUST:

> You, you monster, cannot see
> How this true and loving soul
> For whom faith is her whole
> Being and the only road
> To beatitude, must feel a holy horror
> Having to count her beloved lost for good.

MEPHISTOPHELES:

> You supersensual, sensual buck,
> Led by the nose by the girl you court!

FAUST:

> O you abortion of fire and muck!

MEPHISTOPHELES:

> And she also has skill in physiognomy;
> In my presence she feels she doesn't know what,
> She reads some hidden sense behind my little mask,
> She feels that I am assuredly a genius—
> Maybe the devil if she dared to ask.
> Now: to-night—

FAUST:

> What is to-night to you?

MEPHISTOPHELES:

> I have my pleasure in it too.

AT THE WELL

(Gretchen and Lieschen with pitchers)

LIESCHEN:

Haven't you heard about Barbara? Not what's passed?

GRETCHEN:

Not a word. I go out very little.

LIESCHEN:

It's true, Sibylla told me to-day:
She has made a fool of herself at last.
So much for her fine airs!

GRETCHEN:

Why?

LIESCHEN:

It stinks!
Now she feeds two when she eats and drinks.

GRETCHEN:

Ah!

LIESCHEN:

Yes; she has got her deserts in the end.
What a time she's been hanging on her friend!
Going the rounds
To the dances and the amusement grounds,
She had to be always the first in the line,
He was always standing her cakes and wine;
She thought her looks so mighty fine,
She was so brazen she didn't waver
To take the presents that he gave her.
Such cuddlings and such carryings on—
But now the pretty flower is gone.

GRETCHEN:

Poor thing!

LIESCHEN:

Is that the way you feel?
When we were at the spinning-wheel
And mother kept us upstairs at night,
She was below with her heart's delight;
On the bench or in the shady alley
They never had long enough to dally.
But now she must grovel in the dirt,
Do penance in church in a hair shirt.

GRETCHEN:

But surely he will marry her.

LIESCHEN:

He'd be a fool! A smart young chap
Has plenty of other casks to tap.
Besides he's gone.

GRETCHEN:

That's not right.

LIESCHEN:

If she hooks him she won't get off light!
The boys will tear her wreath in half
And we shall strew her door with chaff.

(*Lieschen goes off*)

GRETCHEN (*going home*):

What scorn I used to pour upon her
When a poor maiden lost her honour!
My tongue could never find a name
Bad enough for another's shame!
I thought it black and I blackened it,
It was never black enough to fit,
And I blessed myself and acted proud—
And now I too am under a cloud.
Yet, God! What drove me to this pass,
It was all so good, so dear, alas!

RAMPARTS

(In a niche in the wall is an image of the Mater Dolorosa. In front of it Gretchen is putting fresh flowers in the pots)

GRETCHEN:

Mary, bow down,
Beneath thy woeful crown,
Thy gracious face on me undone!

The sword in thy heart,
Smart upon smart,
Thou lookest up to thy dear son;

Sending up sighs
To the Father which rise
For His grief and for thine own.

Who can gauge
What torments rage
Through the whole of me and how—
How my poor heart is troubled in me,
How fears and longings undermine me?
Only thou knowest, only thou!

Wherever I may go,
What woe, what woe, what woe
Is growing beneath my heart!
Alas, I am hardly alone,
I moan, I moan, I moan
And my heart falls apart.

The flower-pots in my window
I watered with tears, ah me,
When in the early morning
I picked these flowers for thee.

Not sooner in my bedroom
The sun's first rays were shed
Than I in deepest sorrow
Sat waking on my bed.

Save me from shame and death in one!
Ah, bow down
Thou of the woeful crown,
Thy gracious face on me undone.

NIGHT SCENE AT GRETCHEN'S DOOR

VALENTINE:

When I was at some drinking bout
Where big talk tends to blossom out,
And my companions raised their voice
To praise the maidens of their choice
And drowned their praises in their drink,
Then I would sit and never blink,
Propped on my elbow listening
To all their brags and blustering.
Then smiling I would stroke my beard
And raise the bumper in my hand
And say: 'Each fellow to his taste!
But is there one in all the land
To hold a candle to my own
Dear sister, Gretchen? No, there's none!'
Hear! Hear! Kling! Klang! It went around;
Some cried: 'His judgment is quite sound,
She is the pearl of womanhood!'
That shut those boasters up for good.
And now! It would make one tear one's hair
And run up walls in one's despair!
Each filthy fellow in the place
Can sneer and jeer at my disgrace!
And I, like a man who's deep in debt,
Every chance word must make me sweat.
I could smash their heads for them if I tried—
I could not tell them that they lied.

(Faust and Mephistopheles enter)

VALENTINE:

Who comes there, slinking? Who comes there?
If I mistake not, they're a pair.
If it's he, I'll scrag him on the spot;
He'll be dead before he knows what's what!

FAUST:

>How from the window of the sacristy there
>The undying lamp sends up its little flicker
>Which glimmers sideways weak and weaker
>And round it presses the dark air.
>My heart too feels its night, its noose.

MEPHISTOPHELES:

>And I feel like a tom-cat on the loose,
>Brushing along the fire escape
>And round the walls, a stealthy shape;
>Moreover I feel quite virtuous,
>Just a bit burglarious, a bit lecherous.
>You see, I'm already haunted to the marrow
>By the glorious Walpurgis Night.
>It returns to us the day after to-morrow,
>Then one knows why one's awake all right.

FAUST:

>I'd like some ornament, some ring,
>For my dear mistress. I feel sad
>To visit her without anything.

MEPHISTOPHELES:

>It's really nothing to regret—
>That you needn't pay for what you get.
>Now that the stars are gems on heaven's brocade,
>You shall hear a real masterpiece.
>I will sing her a moral serenade
>That her folly may increase.

>(*He sings to the guitar*)

MEPHISTOPHELES:

>Catherine, my dear,
>What? Waiting here
>At your lover's door
>When the stars of the night are fading?
>Oh don't begin!
>When he lifts the pin,
>A maid goes in—
>But she won't come out a maiden.

So think aright!
Grant him delight
And it's good night,
You poor, poor things—Don't linger!
A girl who's wise
Will hide her prize
From robber's eyes—
Unless she's a ring on her finger.

(*Valentine comes forward*)

VALENTINE:

Damn you! Who're you seducing here?
You damned pied piper! You magician!
First to the devil with your guitar!
Then to the devil with the musician!

MEPHISTOPHELES:

The guitar is finished. Look, it's broken in two.

VALENTINE:

Now then, to break your heads for you!

MEPHISTOPHELES:

Doctor! Courage! All you can muster!
Stick by me and do as I say!
Quick now, draw your feather duster!
I'll parry his blows, so thrust away!

VALENTINE:

Then parry that!

MEPHISTOPHELES:

Why not, why not?

VALENTINE:

And that!

MEPHISTOPHELES:

Of course.

VALENTINE:

Is he the devil or what?
What's this? My hand's already lamed.

MEPHISTOPHELES:
Strike, you!

VALENTINE:

Oh!

(*Valentine falls*)

MEPHISTOPHELES:

Now the lout is tamed!
But we must go! Vanish in the wink of an eye!
They're already raising a murderous hue and cry.

MARTHA (*at the window*):
Come out! Come out!

GRETCHEN (*at the window*):

Bring a light!

MARTHA (*as before*):
There's a row and a scuffle, they're having a fight.

MAN:

Here's one on the ground; he's dead.

MARTHA (*coming out*):
The murderers, have they gone?

GRETCHEN (*coming out*):
Who's here?

MAN:

Your mother's son.

GRETCHEN:
O God! What pain! O God!

VALENTINE:

> I am dying—that's soon said
> And sooner done, no doubt.
> Why do you women stand howling and wailing?
> Come round and hear me out.

> (*They all gather round him*)

> Look, my Gretchen, you're young still,
> You have not yet sufficient skill,
> You bungle things a bit.
> Here is a tip—you need no more—
> Since you are once for all a whore,
> Then make a job of it!

GRETCHEN:

> My brother? O God! Is it I you blame!

VALENTINE:

> Leave our Lord God out of the game!
> What is done I'm afraid is done,
> As one starts one must carry on.
> You began with one man on the sly,
> There will be more of them by and by,
> And when a dozen have done with you
> The whole town will have you too.

> When Shame is born, she first appears
> In this world in secrecy,
> And the veil of night is drawn so tight
> Over her head and ears;
> Yes, people would kill her and forget her.
> But she grows still more and more
> And brazenly roams from door to door
> And yet her appearance grows no better.
> The more her face creates dismay,
> The more she seeks the light of day.
> Indeed I see the time draw on
> When all good people in this town
> Will turn aside from you, you tart,
> As from a corpse in the plague cart.

Then your heart will sink within you,
When they look you in the eye!
It's good-bye to your golden chains!
And church-going and mass—good-bye!
No nice lace collars any more
To make you proud on the dancing floor!
No, in some dark and filthy nook
You'll hide with beggars and crippled folk
And, if God pardon you, he may;
You are cursed on earth till your dying day.

MARTHA:

Commend your soul to the mercy of God!
Will you add slander to your load?

VALENTINE:

If I could get at your withered body,
You bawd, you sinner born and hardened!
Then I should hope that all my sins
And in full measure might be pardoned.

GRETCHEN:

My brother! O hell's misery!

VALENTINE:

I tell you: let your weeping be.
When you and your honour came to part,
It was you that stabbed me to the heart.
I go to God through the sleep of death,
A soldier—brave to his last breath.

(*He dies*)

CATHEDRAL

(Organ and anthem. Gretchen in the congregation. An Evil Spirit whispers to her over her shoulder)

EVIL SPIRIT:

How different it all was
Gretchen, when you came here
All innocent to the altar,
Out of the worn-out little book
Lisping your prayers,
Half a child's game,
Half God in the heart!
Gretchen!
How is your head?
And your heart—
What are its crimes?
Do you pray for your mother's soul, who thanks to you
And your sleeping draught overslept into a long, long
    pain?
And whose blood stains your threshold?
Yes, and already under your heart
Does it not grow and quicken
And torture itself and you
With its foreboding presence?

GRETCHEN:

Alas! Alas!
If I could get rid of the thoughts
Which course through my head hither and thither
Despite me!

CHOIR:

Dies irae, dies illa
Solvet saeclum in favilla.

(The organ plays)

EVIL SPIRIT:

> Agony seizes you!
> The trumpet sounds!
> The graves tremble
> And your heart
> From its ashen rest
> To fiery torment
> Comes up recreated
> Trembling too!

GRETCHEN:

> Oh to escape from here!
> I feel as if the organ
> Were stifling me,
> And the music dissolving
> My heart in its depths.

CHOIR:

> Judex ergo cum sedebit,
> Quidquid latet adparebit,
> Nil inultum remanebit.

GRETCHEN:

> I cannot breathe!
> The pillars of the walls
> Are round my throat!
> The vaulted roof
> Chokes me!—Air!

EVIL SPIRIT:

> Hide yourself! Nor sin nor shame
> Remains hidden.
> Air? Light?
> Woe to you!

CHOIR:

> Quid sum miser tunc dicturus?
> Quem patronum rogaturus?
> Cum vix justus sit securus.

EVIL SPIRIT:

> The blessed turn
> Their faces from you.
> The pure shudder
> To reach out their hands to you.
> Woe!

CHOIR:

> Quid sum miser tunc dicturus?

GRETCHEN:

> Neighbour! Help! Your smelling bottle!
>
> (*She faints*)

WALPURGIS NIGHT

(Faust and Mephistopheles making their way through the Hartz Mountains)

MEPHISTOPHELES:

A broomstick—don't you long for such a conveyance?
I'd find the coarsest he-goat some assistance.
Taking this road, our goal is still in the distance.

FAUST:

No, so long as my legs are not in abeyance,
I can make do with this knotted stick.
What is the use of going too quick?
To creep along each labyrinthine valley,
Then climb this scarp, downwards from which
The bubbling spring makes its eternal sally,
This is the spice that makes such journeys rich.
Already the spring is weaving through the birches,
Even the pine already feels the spring;
Should not our bodies too give it some purchase?

MEPHISTOPHELES:

Candidly—*I* don't feel a thing.
In my body all is winter,
I would prefer a route through frost and snow.
How sadly the imperfect disc
Of the red moon rises with belated glow
And the light it gives is bad, at every step
One runs into some rock or tree!
Permit me to ask a will o' the wisp.
I see one there, he's burning heartily.
Ahoy, my friend! Might I call on you to help us?
Why do you blaze away there to no purpose?
Be so good as to light us along our road.

WILL O' THE WISP:

> I only hope my sense of your mightiness
> Will control my natural flightiness;
> A zigzag course is our accustomed mode.

MEPHISTOPHELES:

> Ha! Ha! So it's men you want to imitate.
> In the name of the Devil you go straight
> Or I'll blow out your flickering, dickering light!

WILL O' THE WISP:

> You're the head of the house, I can see that all right,
> You are welcome to use me at your convenience.
> But remember, the mountain is magic-mad to-day
> And, if a will o' the wisp is to show you the way,
> You too must show a little lenience.

FAUST, MEPHISTOPHELES, WILL O' THE WISP (*singing successively*):

> Into realms of dreams and witchcraft
> We, it seems, have found an ingress.
> Lead us well and show your woodcraft,
> That we may make rapid progress
> Through these wide and desert spaces.
>
> Trees on trees—how each one races,
> Pushing past—how each one hastens!
> And the crags that make obeisance!
> And the rocks with long-nosed faces—
> Hear them snorting, hear them blowing!
>
> Through the stones and lawns are flowing
> Brook and brooklet, downward hustling.
> Is that song—or is it rustling?
> Sweet, sad notes of love—a relic—
> Voices from those days angelic?
> Thus we hope, we love—how vainly!
> Echo like an ancient rumour
> Calls again, yes, calls back plainly.
>
> Now—Tu-whit!—we near the purlieu
> Of—Tu-whoo!—owl, jay and curlew;

Are they all in waking humour?
In the bushes are those lizards—
Straggling legs and bloated gizzards?
And the roots like snakes around us
Coil from crag and sandy cranny,
Stretch their mad and strange antennae
Grasping at us to confound us;
Stretch from gnarled and living timber
Towards the passer-by their limber
Polyp-suckers!
      And in legions
Through these mossy, heathy regions
Mice, all colours, come cavorting!
And above, a serried cohort,
Fly the glow-worms as our escort—
More confusing than escorting.

Tell me what our real case is!
Are we stuck or are we going?
Rocks and trees, they all seem flying
Round and round and making faces,
And the will o' the wisps are blowing
Up so big and multiplying.

MEPHISTOPHELES:

Hold my coat-tails, hold on tight!
Standing on this central height
Marvelling see how far and wide
Mammon lights the peaks inside.

FAUST:

How strangely through the mountain hollows
A sad light gleams as of morning-red
And like a hound upon the scent
Probes the gorges' deepest bed!
Here fumes arise, there vapours float,
Here veils of mist catch sudden fire
Which creeps along, a flimsy thread,
Then fountains up, a towering spire.
Here a whole stretch it winds its way
With a hundred veins throughout the glen,

And here in the narrow neck of the pass
Is suddenly one strand again.
There, near by, are dancing sparks
Sprinkled around like golden sand.
But look! The conflagration climbs
The crags' full height, hand over hand.

MEPHISTOPHELES:

Does not Sir Mammon light his palace
In splendid style for this occasion?
You are lucky to have seen it;
Already I sense the noisy guests' invasion.

FAUST:

How the Wind Hag rages through the air!
What blows she rains upon the nape of my neck!

MEPHISTOPHELES:

You must clamp yourself to the ancient ribs of the rock
Or she'll hurl you into this gorge, to find your grave down
    there.
A mist is thickening the night.
Hark to the crashing of the trees!
The owls are flying off in fright.
And the ever-green palaces—
Hark to their pillars sundering!
Branches moaning and breaking!
Tree-trunks mightily thundering!
Roots creaking and yawning!
Tree upon tree in appalling
Confusion crashing and falling,
And through the wreckage on the scarps
The winds are hissing and howling.
Do you hear those voices in the air?
Far-off voices? Voices near?
Aye, the whole length of the mountain side
The witch-song streams in a crazy tide.

WITCHES (*in chorus*):

    The witches enter the Brocken scene,
    The stubble is yellow, the corn is green.

There assembles the mighty horde,
Urian sits aloft as lord.
So we go—over stock and stone—
Farting witch on stinking goat.

A VOICE:

But ancient Baubo comes alone,
She rides on a mother sow—take note.

CHORUS:

So honour to whom honour is due!
Let Mother Baubo head the queue!
A strapping sow and Mother on top
And we'll come after, neck and crop.

The way is broad, the way is long,
How is this for a crazy throng?
The pitchfork pricks, the broomstick pokes,
The mother bursts and the child chokes.

VOICE FROM ABOVE:
Come along, come along, from Felsensee!

VOICES FROM BELOW:
We'd like to mount with you straight away.
We wash ourselves clean behind and before
But we are barren for evermore.

CHORUS:

The wind is silent, the star's in flight,
The sad moon hides herself from sight.
The soughing of the magic choir
Scatters a thousand sparks of fire.

VOICE FROM BELOW:
Wait! Wait!

VOICE FROM ABOVE:
Who calls there from the cleft in the rock?

VOICE FROM BELOW:

>Don't leave me behind! Don't leave me behind!
>Three hundred years I've been struggling up
>And I can never reach the top;
>I want to be with my own kind.

CHORUS:

>Ride on a broom or ride on a stick,
>Ride on a fork or a goat—but quick!
>Who cannot to-night achieve the climb
>Is lost and damned till the end of time.

HALF-WITCH:

>So long, so long, I've been on the trot;
>How far ahead the rest have got!
>At home I have neither peace nor cheer
>And yet I do not find it here.

CHORUS:

>Their ointment makes the witches hale,
>A rag will make a decent sail
>And any trough a ship for flight;
>You'll never fly, if not to-night.
>Once at the peak, you circle round
>And then you sweep along the ground
>And cover the heath far and wide—
>Witchhood in swarms on every side.

>>(*The Witches land*)

MEPHISTOPHELES:

>What a push and a crush and a rush and a clatter!
>How they sizzle and whisk, how they babble and batter!
>Kindle and sparkle and blaze and stink!
>A true witch-element, I think.
>Only stick to me or we shall be swept apart!
>Where are you?

FAUST:

>Here!

MEPHISTOPHELES:

What! Carried so far already!
I must show myself the master on this ground.
Room! Here comes Voland! Room, sweet rabble! Steady!
Here, Doctor, catch hold of me. Let's make one bound
Out of this milling crowd and so get clear.
Even for the likes of me it's *too* mad here.
There's something yonder casting a peculiar glare,
Something attracts me towards those bushes.
Come with me! We will slip in there.

FAUST:

You spirit of contradiction! Go on though! I'll follow.
You have shown yourself a clever fellow. Quite!
We visit the Brocken on Walpurgis Night
To shut ourselves away in this lonely hollow!

MEPHISTOPHELES:

Only look—what motley flames!
It's a little club for fun and games
One's not alone with a few, you know.

FAUST:

I'd rather be above there though.
Already there's fire and whorls of smoke.
The Prince of Evil is drawing the folk;
Many a riddle must there be solved.

MEPHISTOPHELES:

And many a new one too evolved.
Let the great world, if it likes, run riot;
We will set up here in quiet.
It is a custom of old date
To make one's own small worlds within the great.
I see young witches here, bare to the buff,
And old ones dressed—wisely enough.
If only for my sake, do come on;
It's little trouble and great fun.
I hear some music being let loose too.
What a damned clack! It's what one must get used to.

Come along! Come along! You have no choice.
I'll lead the way and sponsor you
And you'll be obliged to me anew.
What do you say? This milieu isn't small.
Just look! You can see no end to it at all.
A hundred fires are blazing in a row;
They dance and gossip and cook and drink and court—
Tell me where there is better sport!

FAUST:

Do you intend, to introduce us here,
To play the devil or the sorcerer?

MEPHISTOPHELES:

I am quite accustomed to go incognito
But one wears one's orders on gala days, you know.
I have no garter for identification
But my cloven foot has here some reputation.
See that snail? Creeping up slow and steady?
Her sensitive feelers have already
Sensed out something odd in me.
Here I could *not* hide my identity.
But come! Let us go the round of the fires
And I'll play go-between to your desires.

COSTER-WITCH:

Gentlemen, don't pass me by!
Don't miss your opportunity!
Inspect my wares with careful eye;
I have a great variety.
And yet there is nothing on my stall
Whose like on earth you could not find,
That in its time has done no small
Harm to the world and to mankind.
No dagger which has not drunk of blood,
No goblet which has not poured its hot and searing
Poison into some healthy frame,
No gewgaw which has not ruined some endearing
Woman, no sword which has not been used to hack
A bond in two and stab a partner in the back.

MEPHISTOPHELES:

> Auntie! You are behind the times,
> Past and done with! Past and done!
> You must go in for novelties!
> You'll lose our custom if you've none.

FAUST:

> I mustn't go crazy unawares!
> This is a fair to end all fairs.

MEPHISTOPHELES:

> The whole crowd's forcing its way above;
> You find you're shoved though you may think you shove.

FAUST:

> Who then is that?

MEPHISTOPHELES:

> Look well at Madam;
> That's Lilith.

FAUST:

> Who?

MEPHISTOPHELES:

> First wife of Adam.
> Be on your guard against her lovely hair,
> That shining ornament which has no match;
> Any young man whom those fair toils can catch,
> She will not quickly loose him from her snare.

FAUST:

> Look, an old and a young one, there they sit.
> They have already frisked a bit.

MEPHISTOPHELES:

> No rest to-night for 'em, not a chance.
> They're starting again. Come on! Let's join the dance.

> *(Faust dances with a young witch)*

FAUST:

> A lovely dream once came to me
> In which I saw an apple tree,
> On which two lovely apples shine,
> They beckon me, I start to climb.

YOUNG WITCH:

> Those little fruit you long for so
> Just as in Eden long ago.
> Joy runs through me, through and through;
> My garden bears its apples too.

(Faust breaks away from the dance)

MEPHISTOPHELES:

> Why did you let that lovely maiden go
> Who danced with you and so sweetly sang?

FAUST:

> Ugh, in the middle of it there sprang
> Out of her mouth a little red mouse.

MEPHISTOPHELES:

> Why complain? That's nothing out of the way;
> You should be thankful it wasn't grey.
> In an hour of love! What a senseless grouse!

FAUST:

> And then I saw—

MEPHISTOPHELES:

> What?

FAUST:

> Mephisto, look over there!
> Do you see a girl in the distance, pale and fair?
> Who drags herself, only slowly, from the place?
> And seems to walk with fetters on her feet?
> I must tell you that I think I see
> Something of dear Gretchen in her face.

MEPHISTOPHELES:

> That can do no one good! Let it alone! Beware!
> It is a lifeless phantom, an image of air.
> It is a bad thing to behold;
> Its cold look makes the blood of man run cold,
> One turns to stone almost upon the spot;
> You have heard of Medusa, have you not?

FAUST:

> Indeed, they are the eyes of one who is dead,
> Unclosed by loving hands, left open, void.
> That is the breast which Gretchen offered me,
> And that is the sweet body I enjoyed.

MEPHISTOPHELES:

> That is mere magic, you gullible fool! She can
> Appear in the shape of his love to every man.

FAUST:

> What ravishment! What pain! Oh stay!
> That look! I cannot turn away!
> How strange that that adorable neck
> In one red thread should be arrayed
> As thin as the back of a knife-blade.

MEPHISTOPHELES:

> You are quite correct! I see it too.
> She can also carry her head under her arm,
> Perseus has cut it off for her.
> Always this love of things untrue!

> (*A choir is heard, pianissimo*)

CHOIR:

> Drifting cloud and gauzy mist
> Brighten and dissever.
> Breeze on the leaf and wind in the reeds
> And all is gone for ever.

DREARY DAY—OPEN COUNTRY

FAUST:

In misery! In despair! Long on the earth a wretched wanderer, now a prisoner! A criminal cooped in a dungeon for horrible torments, that dear and luckless creature! To end so! So! Perfidious, worthless spirit—and this you have kept from me!

Stand! Just stand there! Roll your devilish eyes spitefully round in your head! Stand and brave me with your unbearable presence! A prisoner! In irremediable misery! Abandoned to evil spirits, to judging, unfeeling man! And I in the meantime—you lull me with stale diversions, you hide her worsening plight from me, you abandon her to perdition!

MEPHISTOPHELES:

She is not the first.

FAUST:

Dog! Loathsome monster! Change him, Thou eternal Spirit! Change this serpent back to his shape of a dog, in which he often delighted to trot before me at night—to roll about at the feet of the harmless wanderer and, as he tripped, to sink his teeth in his shoulders. Change him back to his fancy-shape that he may crouch in the sand on his belly before me, that I may trample over his vileness!

Not the first, you say! O the pity of it! What human soul can grasp that more than one creature has sunk to the depth of this misery, that the first did not pay off the guilt of all the rest, writhing and racked in death before the eyes of the Ever-Pardoning! It pierces me to my marrow and core, the torment of this one girl —and you grin calmly at the fate of thousands!

MEPHISTOPHELES:

Now we're already back at our wits' end—the point where your human intelligence snaps. Why do you enter our company, if you can't carry it through? So you want to fly—and have no head for heights? Did we force ourselves on you—or you on us?

FAUST:

Do not bare at me so those greedy fangs of yours! You sicken me! O great and glorious Spirit, Thou who didst deign to appear to me, Thou who knowest my heart and my soul, why fetter me to this odious partner who grazes on mischief and laps up destruction?

MEPHISTOPHELES:

Have you finished?

FAUST:

Save her! Or woe to you! The most withering curse upon you for thousands of years!

MEPHISTOPHELES:

I cannot undo the avenger's bonds, his bolts I cannot open. Save her! Who was it plunged her into ruin? I or you?

(Faust looks wildly around)

MEPHISTOPHELES:

Are you snatching at the thunder? Luckily, that is forbidden you wretched mortals. To smash to pieces his innocent critic, that is the way the tyrant relieves himself when in difficulties.

FAUST:

Bring me to her! She shall be free!

MEPHISTOPHELES:

And what of the risk you will run? Let me tell you; the town is still tainted with blood-guilt from your hand. Over the site of the murder there float avenging spirits who await the returning murderer.

FAUST:

That too from *you*? Murder and death of a world on your monstrous head! Take me to her, I tell you; set her free!

MEPHISTOPHELES:

I will take you, and what I *can* do—listen! Am I omnipotent in heaven and earth? I will cast a cloud on the gaoler's senses; do you get hold of the keys and carry her out with your own human hands. I meanwhile wait, my magic horses are ready, I carry you off. That much I can manage.

FAUST:

Away! Away!

NIGHT

(Faust and Mephistopheles fly past on black horses)

FAUST:

What do they weave round the Gallows Rock?

MEPHISTOPHELES:

Can't tell what they're cooking and hatching.

FAUST:

Floating up, floating down, bending, descending.

MEPHISTOPHELES:

A witch corporation.

FAUST:

Black mass, black water.

MEPHISTOPHELES:

Come on! Come on!

DUNGEON

(Faust with a bunch of keys and a lamp, in front of an iron door)

FAUST:

A long unwonted trembling seizes me,
The woe of all mankind seizes me fast.
It is here she lives, behind these dripping walls,
Her crime was but a dream too good to last!
And *you*, Faust, waver at the door?
You fear to see your love once more?
Go in at once—or her hope of life is past.

(He tries the key. Gretchen starts singing inside)

GRETCHEN:

My mother, the whore,
Who took my life!
My father, the rogue,
Who ate my flesh!
My little sister
My bones did lay
In a cool, cool glen;
And there I turned to a pretty little wren;
Fly away! Fly away!

(Faust opens the lock)

FAUST:

She does not suspect that her lover is listening—
To the chains clanking, the straw rustling.

(He enters)

GRETCHEN:

Oh! They come! O death! It's hard! Hard!

FAUST:

Quiet! I come to set you free.

(She throws herself at his feet)

GRETCHEN:

If you are human, feel my misery.

FAUST:

Do not cry out—you will wake the guard.

(He takes hold of the chains to unlock them)

GRETCHEN *(on her knees)*:

Who has given you this power,
Hangman, so to grieve me?
To fetch me at this midnight hour!
Have pity! Oh reprieve me!
Will to-morrow not serve when the bells are rung?

(She gets up)

I am still so young, I am still so young!
Is my death so near?
I was pretty too, that was what brought me here.
My lover was by, he's far to-day;
My wreath lies torn, my flowers have been thrown away.
Don't seize on me so violently!
What have I done to you? Let me be!
Let me not vainly beg and implore;
You know I have never seen you before.

FAUST:

Can I survive this misery?

GRETCHEN:

I am now completely in your power.
Only let me first suckle my child.
This night I cherished it, hour by hour;
To torture me they took it away
And now I murdered it, so they say.
And I shall never be happy again.

People make ballads about me—the heartless crew!
An old story ends like this—
Must mine too?

(*Faust throws himself on the ground*)

FAUST:

Look! At your feet a lover lies
To loose you from your miseries.

(*Gretchen throws herself beside him*)

GRETCHEN:

O, let us call on the saints on bended knee!
Beneath these steps—but see—
Beneath this sill
The cauldron of Hell!
And within,
The Evil One in his fury
Raising a din!

FAUST:

Gretchen! Gretchen!

GRETCHEN:

That was my lover's voice!

(*She springs up; the chains fall off*)

I heard him calling. Where can he be?
No one shall stop me. I am free!
Quick! My arms round his neck!
And lie upon his bosom! Quick!
He called 'Gretchen!' He stood at the door.
Through the whole of Hell's racket and roar,
Through the threats and jeers and from far beyond
I heard that voice so sweet, so fond.

FAUST:

It is I!

GRETCHEN:

It's you? Oh say so once again!

(*She clasps him*)

It is! It is! Where now is all my pain?
And where the anguish of my captivity?
It's you; you have come to rescue me!
I am saved!
The street is back with me straight away
Where I saw you that first day,
And the happy garden too
Where Martha and I awaited you.

FAUST:

Come! Come!

GRETCHEN:

Oh stay with me, oh do!
Where *you* stay, I would like to, too.

FAUST:

Hurry!
If you don't,
The penalty will be sore.

GRETCHEN:

What! Can you kiss no more?
So short an absence, dear, as this
And you've forgotten how to kiss!
Why do I feel so afraid, clasping your neck?
In the old days your words, your looks,
Were a heavenly flood I could not check
And you kissed me as if you would smother me—
Kiss me now!
Or I'll kiss you!

(She kisses him)

Oh your lips are cold as stone!
And dumb!
What has become
Of your love?
Who has robbed me of my own?

(She turns away from him)

FAUST:

>Come! Follow me, my love! Be bold!
>I will cherish you after a thousandfold.
>Only follow me now! That is all I ask of you.

GRETCHEN:

>And is it you then? Really? Is it true?

FAUST:

>It is! But come!

GRETCHEN:

>You are undoing each chain,
>You take me to your arms again.
>How comes it you are not afraid of me?
>Do you know, my love, *whom* you are setting free?

FAUST:

>Come! The deep night is passing by and beyond.

GRETCHEN:

>My mother, I have murdered her;
>I drowned my child in the pond.
>Was it not a gift to you and me?
>To you too—You! Are you what you seem?
>Give me your hand! It is not a dream!
>Your dear hand—but, oh, it's wet!
>Wipe it off! I think
>There is blood on it.
>Oh God! What have you done?
>Put up your sword,
>I beg you to.

FAUST:

>Let what is gone be gone!
>You are killing me.

GRETCHEN:

>No! *You* must live on!
>I will tell you about the graves—
>You must get them put right

At morning light;
Give the best place to my mother,
The one next door to my brother,
Me a shade to the side—
A gap, but not too wide.
And the little one on my right breast.
No one else shall share my rest.
When it was you, when I could clasp you,
That was a sweet, a lovely day!
But I no longer can attain it,
I feel I must use force to grasp you,
As if you were thrusting me away.
And yet it's you and you look so kind, so just.

FAUST:

If you feel it's I, then come with me! You must!

GRETCHEN:

Outside there?

FAUST:

Into the air!

GRETCHEN:

If the grave is there
And death on the watch, then come!
Hence to the final rest of the tomb
And not a step beyond—
You are going now? O Heinrich, if *I* could too!

FAUST:

You can! The door is open. Only respond!

GRETCHEN:

I dare not go out; for me there is no more hope.
They are lying in wait for me; what use is flight?
To have to beg, it is so pitiable
And that with a conscience black as night!
So pitiable to tramp through foreign lands—
And in the end I must fall into their hands!

FAUST:

> I shall stay by you.

GRETCHEN:

> Be quick! Be quick!
> Save your poor child!
> Go! Straight up the path—
> Along by the brook—
> Over the bridge—
> Into the wood—
> Left where the plank is—
> In the pond!
> Catch hold of it quickly!
> It's trying to rise,
> It's kicking still!
> Save it! Save it!

FAUST:

> Collect yourself!
> One step—just one—and you are free.

GRETCHEN:

> If only we were past the hill!
> There sits my mother on a stone—
> My brain goes cold and dead—
> There sits my mother on a stone—
> And wags and wags her head.
> No sign, no nod, her head is such a weight
> She'll wake no more, she slept so late.
> She slept that we might sport and play.
> What a time that was of holiday!

FAUST:

> If prayer and argument are no resource,
> I will risk saving you by force.

GRETCHEN:

> No! I will have no violence! Let me go!
> Don't seize me in that murderous grip!
> I have done everything else for you, you know.

FAUST:

My love! My love! The day is dawning!

GRETCHEN:

Day! Yes, it's growing day! The last day breaks on me!
My wedding day it was to be!
Tell no one you had been before with Gretchen.
Alas for my garland!
There's no more chance!
We shall meet again—
But not at the dance.
The people are thronging—but silently;
Street and square
Cannot hold them there.
The bell tolls—it tolls for *me*.
How they seize me, bind me, like a slave!
Already I'm swept away to the block.
Already there jabs at every neck,
The sharp blade which jabs at mine.
The world lies mute as the grave.

FAUST:

I wish I had never been born!

(*Mephistopheles appears outside*)

MEPHISTOPHELES:

Away! Or you are lost.
Futile wavering! Waiting and prating!
My horses are shivering,
The dawn's at the door.

GRETCHEN:

What rises up from the floor?
It's he! Send him away! It's he!
What does he want in the holy place?
It is I he wants!

FAUST:

You shall live!

GRETCHEN:

> Judgment of God! I have given myself to Thee!

MEPHISTOPHELES (*to Faust*):

> Come! Or I'll leave you both in the lurch.

GRETCHEN:

> O Father, save me! I am Thine!
> You angels! Hosts of the Heavenly Church,
> Guard me, stand round in serried line!
> Heinrich! I shudder to look at you.

MEPHISTOPHELES:

> She is condemned!

VOICE FROM ABOVE:

> Redeemed!

MEPHISTOPHELES:

> Follow me!

> (*He vanishes with Faust*)

VOICE (*from within, dying away*):

> Heinrich! Heinrich!

FAUST

PART 2

ACT I

*

A PLEASANT LANDSCAPE

Faust, bedded on flowery turf, tired, restless, trying to sleep

TWILIGHT
Graceful little spirits hover in a circle around him.
Ariel's song is accompanied by Aeolian harps.

ARIEL:

> When the vernal showers of blossom
> Drift and shaft on all the earth,
> When the fields' green benediction
> Gleams on all that there had birth,
> Little elves of lofty spirit
> Run to help where help they can,
> Be he holy, be he evil,
> In pity for the luckless man.

You who float round this head in airy circles,
Show him the kindness of the noble elf,
Assuage the strife that makes his heart aghast,
Fend off the poisoned shafts of the mind that blames itself,
And cleanse his soul from the horror of his past!
Night has four phases in her flow;
Now fill them with your friendship, do not tarry!
First lay his head on cushions cool and low,
Then bathe him in the dew from Lethe's source;
The cramped and stiffened body soon grows supple
As it rests to face the day, regains its force.
Your fairest task, ply it aright:
Restore him to the sacred light.

CHORUS OF ELVES:

Serenade

When the air comes warmly wafting
Round the green-invested plains,
Veils of mist and twilight perfumes
Sweetly drop as daylight wanes;
Rock his heart as in a cradle,
Sweetly whisper songs of peace,
And upon his weary eyelids
Close the gates—let daylight cease.

Notturno

Night already has descended
Holy star joins holy star,
Luminaries great and little
Glitter near and gleam afar;
Glitter here in lakes reflected,
Gleam aloft in limpid night;
While the full moon seals the sleeper
Deep with sovereign pomp of light.

Mattutino

Now the hours have been extinguished,
Weal and woe are swept away.
Feel ahead! Your ills are ended,
Trust the new appearing day!
Vales are greening, hills are swelling,
Clumps of shadow and repose;
And the corn in silver ripples
Towards a golden harvest flows.

Reveil

Wish on wish, if you would win them,
Yonder watch the burst of day!
The husk of sleep is only lightly
Round you—Cast the husk away!
Common folk may drag and dally;
You be speedy, you be bold!
The world is for the lofty spirit
Dare he know it and take hold.

(A tremendous noise heralds the approach of the sun)

ARIEL:

Hearken! Hark to the storm of the hours!
Ringing out for spirits' ears
Now the new-born day appears.
Doors of granite clang and toll,
The sun's wheels rattle as they roll,
To what clangour dawn gives rein!
Drums and trumpets far resounding,
Dazzling, deafening, dumbfounding,
Things unheard should so remain.
Into bells of blossom creep,·
Lie there quiet, deep and deep,
Into rock and under leaf;
If it strike you, you are deaf.

FAUST (*waking*):

Life's pulses beat, fresh and alive and royal,
Beneath these skies of dawn they kindly greet;
You, Earth, through this night also you were loyal
And breathe forth resurrection at my feet,
Beginning so soon to clasp me round with pleasure,
Stirring and summoning a strong resolve
Ever to strive for life in highest measure.
Already the world lies opened up in the dawn,
The woods resound with a thousand living voices;
In and out of this glen a ribbon of mist is drawn
But heaven's light probes the hollows however deep
And bough and branch, quickened anew, come sprouting
From the scented cavern where they drowned in sleep;
And colour too upon colour comes from the grey
Where leaf and petal drip with quivering pearls—
A paradise forms around me here to-day.

Look up at the peaks! Behold their annunciation
Of that most solemn hour—for now unfurls
The eternal light, their early perquisite,
Which moves down later to our lower station.
And now the alpine pastures, slopes of green,
Are blessed with the sharp sheen of renovation,
That step by step its downward course advances—

The sun strides forth! and, already dazed, I turn
My smarting eyes aside from his fierce glances.

So is it too when hope by yearning hounded
Trusts and thrusts for its highest goal and chances
To find the gates wing-open, the field unbounded;
But now there bursts from that eternal porch
A superabundance of flame, we stand confounded;
Our aim was life, we wished to light the torch,
And a sea of fire laps round us—beyond measure!
Is it love? Or hate? Which burn and turn about us
In monstrous changing tides of pain and pleasure,
So that we look again to earth to shroud us
In that cloak of youth which is earth's oldest treasure.

Let then the sun remain at my back behind me!
The waterfall the crag sends downward roaring
I watch with a growing joy, a joy to blind me:
Now from fall to fall it rolls in a thousand
And now in tens of thousand streamlets pouring
While jets of spray on spray go skyward soaring.
And yet how nobly from this plash and pelting
The changing permanence of the rainbow flowers,
Now clearly drawn, now into vapour melting,
Spreading around it cool and fragrant showers.
This bow will serve to image man's endeavour.
Think on it and you grasp what lot is ours:
Reflected colour forms our life for ever.

THE IMPERIAL COURT

EMPEROR:

> I greet my dear and loyal subjects
> Assembled here from far and near;
> I see my sages by my throne
> But why does my jester not appear?

FIRST JUNKER:

> Just behind your mantle's sweep
> He fell on the staircase in a heap;
> They lugged the hulking guts away—
> Dead or drunk? One cannot say.

SECOND JUNKER:

> At once with wondrous turn of pace
> Another's pushing for his place.
> Dressed up regardless of expense
> But so grotesque—it gives offence;
> The guard, at pains to disallow
> His entrance, hold their halberds crossed—
> The pushing fool, here he is now!

MEPHISTOPHELES (*kneeling before the throne*):

> What is accursed and always welcome?
> Desired and always hounded out?
> What is continually protected?
> A butt for all to blame and flout?
> Whom do you fear to call to audience?
> Whose name brings joy to every heart?
> What is it that draws near your throne?
> Banned by itself to keep apart?

EMPEROR:

> Spare your words for this occasion,
> Your riddles here must needs fall flat,

That is the business of these gentry—
You solve theirs! I'd welcome that.
My old fool's flown, I fear, to the Far Away;
Take his place by me. You're my fool to-day!

(*Mephistopheles rises and takes his place on the left*)

MURMURS FROM THE CROWD:
A new jester—
      A new canker—
Where did he come from?
      How did he enter?
The old one fell—
      And he won't wake!
He was a hogshead—
      This is a rake!

EMPEROR:

And therefore, dear and loyal subjects,
You are welcome all from near and far!
You meet when our fortunes are assured
In the skies above us by a propitious star.
But tell me why at this time, why,
When we are set to banish care
And carnival costume is the wear
And we only craved some recreation—
Why must we plague ourselves with deliberation?
But since you believe that nothing else can be done,
We must confer, so let's get on!

CHANCELLOR:

The highest virtue, haloed from above
Circles the Emperor's head and only he
Can exercise it with authority:
Justice! Justice the boon that all men love,
Claim and desire and scarcely do without,
It lies with him to dispense it through the land.
But oh! Can understanding help man's spirit,
Goodness his heart or willingness his hand,
When through the state a feverish mania storms
And evil hatches in all evil forms?

Who looks down from this room, this court supreme,
On the wide realm will think it a bad dream,
Where the misshapen rules in misshapen-ness,
And lawlessness holds the field in legal dress,
And a whole world unfolds of truthlessness.

One rustles cattle, one a wife,
Cup, cross and candle from the altar,
And boasts about it many a year,
Skin free of scratch and neck of halter.
New plaintiffs throng to law, the judge
Parades his high—and soft—position,
While in repulsive turmoil sways
The waxing tumult of sedition.
He dares to brag of crime and scandal,
Who has an accomplice in the court,
While you can hear the cry of Guilty
Where innocence is its own support.
Thus all the world is breaking up,
Sweeping all order out of sight;
Then how can that high sense develop
Which only leads to what is right?
A well-intentioned man must bow
To bribes and flattery in the end;
The judge who cannot punish crime
Will make the criminal his friend.
I paint it black; I should be glad
To veil more thickly work so bad.

Measures *must* be passed ere long;
When all men do and suffer wrong,
Even the Crown is up for loot.

COMMANDER-IN-CHIEF:

What days of madness and disorder!
Everyone kills, is killed to boot,
And nobody obeys an order.
The bourgeois safe behind his walls,
And in his rocky nest the laird
They all conspired to brave us out
And keep their forces unimpaired.

My mercenaries grow impatient
And fret and clamour for their pay,
And did we not still owe them something
They would be off without delay.
He who forbids what all desire
Has stirred a wasps' nest with his hand;
The realm which they were pledged to aid,
The realm lies plundered and unmanned.
We let their madness rage and rule,
Already half the world is lost;
We still have vassal kings abroad—
To none of whom it occurs to share the cost.

TREASURER:

Who boasts of that entente to-day!
The subsidies they swore to pay
Remain like a water-pipe gone dry.
And, sire, throughout your wide domains
Who are the men who've made the gains?
There's a new master every house you try
Who wants to live in independence—
And we must wait and see it done;
We have surrendered so many rights already
That not a right remains to us; not one.
As for the parties as they're called,
Let them praise or let them blame—
There's no relying on them now,
Their love and hate is all the same.
They hide themselves and rest themselves,
Ghibelline no less than Guelf.
Who nowadays will help his neighbour?
Every man is for himself.
They barricade the golden doors,
Everyone scrapes and scoops and stores,
Yet nothing fills the public purse.

STEWARD:

My report too is more than grave.
Every day we want to save
And every day our needs grow worse.
And day by day *my* cares increase.

The *cooks* are troubled by no shortage;
Wild boars and stags and hares and does,
Hens and guinea-hens, ducks and geese,
Their quotas, regular dividends,
Come in all right, one needn't doubt.
But in the end the wine runs out.
Once in the cellar vats were heaped on vats
Of the best vintages and years,
But now the last drop has been drained
By our eternally swilling aristocrats.
And the Town Council too are quite unable
To save their stock—men snatch at pint and pipkin,
And the banquet lies beneath the table.
Now I must count out all I owe,
The Jew will never let me go
But gives advances which instead
Devour my purse for years ahead.
One cannot fatten up one's stock,
The bolster from the bed's in hock,
And at table one is served fore-eaten bread.

EMPEROR:

Tell me, my fool: have *you* no tears to shed?

MEPHISTOPHELES:

I? Not the least. To see the surrounding splendour
Of you and yours—Could confidence be lacking
Where majesty claims unquestioning obedience,
With force prepared to send opponents packing?
Where a good will that a good mind keeps steady
And energy, manifold, are ever ready?
What forces of disaster could unite
To cloud a court where stars like *this* are bright?

MURMURS FROM THE CROWD:

He is a rogue—
        He knows the ropes—
Lies himself in—
        For he has hopes—
I see his game—
        What's in his mind—

And deep in it—
> A scheme, you'll find.

MEPHISTOPHELES:

> Where is there not some deficit in this world?
> There this, there that, but here our lack is gold.
> You can't sweep it up from the floor, oh dear me no,
> But wisdom knows how to tap the depths below.
> For mountains' veins and walls' foundations hold—
> There for the finding—coined and uncoined gold.
> And as for digging it up, you know who can?
> The nature and spirit of a gifted man.

CHANCELLOR:

> Nature and spirit—Spare our Christian ears!
> Atheists are burned for that.
> Such talk inspires the most deep-founded fears.
> Nature is sin, spirit's the devil,
> Between them they cherish scepticism,
> Misshapen child of either evil.
> Not so with us! Our ancient borders
> Of Empire honour but two orders,
> Staunch props of the Imperial Throne—
> Those of religion and chivalry;
> They stand against all storms and take
> Church and State for salary.
> But the mob-mind of muddled spirits
> Allows the rise of an opposition:
> The heretics! The witch-doctors!
> Who are the state's and realm's perdition.
> And these you now in impudent sport
> Will conjure up in our high court;
> Being a fool, you know your kindred
> And feed on their corrupt ambition.

MEPHISTOPHELES:

> Ah, now I know the learned gentleman!
> What you don't touch is miles beyond your scan,
> What you don't grasp is utterly lost to you,
> What you don't calculate you think untrue,
> What you don't weigh you find devoid of weight,
> What you don't mint—that you invalidate.

EMPEROR:

> This does not cancel our deficiency;
> What is the point of your lenten homily?
> I have had my fill of this endless How and When.
> We need gold? All right. Procure it then.

MEPHISTOPHELES:

> I will procure all that you want and more;
> Easy enough—but there's hard work in store;
> The gold is there already—but how to win it,
> That is the job—who's fitted to begin it?
> Yet only think: in those years of desperation
> When floods of invaders drowned both land and nation
> How many a man in his extreme alarm
> Hid here or there his favourite goods from harm.
> In the days of mighty Rome that was the way
> And up till yesterday—and till to-day.
> And all of that the soil still holds concealed;
> The soil's the Emperor's, *he* should have its yield.

TREASURER:

> For a fool, he puts a sensible point of view;
> That is indeed our ancient Emperor's due.

CHANCELLOR:

> Satan is laying golden traps to try us;
> This does not square with what is right and pious.

STEWARD:

> Granted he brings to court such prized donations,
> I'd gladly lump a few slight aberrations.

COMMANDER-IN-CHIEF:

> Smart fool! He promises what all desire;
> But where it comes from, soldiers won't inquire.[1]

---

[1] The thousand lines which follow are omitted in this translation. When our next scene starts the Emperor is already enriched—by the invention of paper money.

PLEASURE GARDEN

(Morning sun)

EMPEROR:

> What a good fortune brought you to my sight,
> Directly out of some Arabian Night!
> If you are fruitful Scheherazade's equal,
> My highest favour is the certain sequel.
> Be always ready when the daily grind,
> As often happens, nauseates my mind.

STEWARD (*entering in haste*):

> Your Imperial Majesty, I never dreamt
> To bring you news so totally exempt
> From care as these which fill me with delight
> And send me into raptures in your sight:
> Bill after bill has now been paid,
> The usurer's demands allayed,
> I'm free of such a hell of care;
> Heaven can't be more debonair.

COMMANDER-IN-CHIEF:

> My soldiers have been paid their due,
> Have signed on all of 'em anew,
> The yeomanry are like new men,
> And whores and landlords breathe again.

EMPEROR:

> How your breast and lungs expand!
> The wrinkled face grows smooth and bland!
> You enter with such eagerness.

TREASURER:

> Ask these two. It is they who managed this.

FAUST:

It is the Chancellor's business to explain.

CHANCELLOR:

In my old age I have been freed from pain.
Listen and look at this portentous bill
Which has made welfare out of all our ill.
(reading) 'Be it known to all men who may so require:
This note is worth a thousand crowns entire.
Which has its guarantee and counterfoil
In untold wealth beneath Imperial soil.
And this hereby is a substitute approved
Until such time as the treasure can be moved.'

EMPEROR:

And do my people think it negotiable?
Do army and court take it for pay in full?
Strange though I think it, I must ratify it.

STEWARD:

To collect those fluttering notes, one couldn't try it;
Once issued, they are scattered in a flash.
The Exchanges stand wide open for the queue
Where every bill is honoured and changed for cash—
Silver and gold—at a discount, it is true.
And then to butcher, baker, pub it goes,
Half the world only seems to think of stuffing;
While the other half in brand new clothes goes puffing.
The clothier cuts the cloth, the tailor sews.
'Long live the Emperor!' makes the cellars gush
In a cooking, roasting, platter-clattering crush.

MEPHISTOPHELES:

Who walks alone along the terraces
Beholds his fairest in a queenly dress,
Hiding behind a splendid peacock fan
With an eye on the bill she smiles upon the man;
More quickly than by wit or oratory
He wins the entrée to her sanctuary.
There's no need now to fuss with pouch or purse,
One's bosom finds this paper light to nurse,

It pairs up snugly with a billet doux.
A breviary can revere and hold it too,
While the soldier, loath to let occasion slip,
Can quickly ease the belt upon his hip.
Excuse me if such low examples seem
To depreciate a work of high esteem.

FAUST:

The excess of treasure frozen in your lands,
Deep in the soil awaiting human hands,
Lies there unused. The furthest range of thought
Cannot define such riches as it ought;
And fancy in her highest, wildest flight
Exerts herself and never guesses right.
But penetrating spirits will transmit
Infinite trust in what is infinite.

MEPHISTOPHELES:

In lieu of gold and pearls this paper note
Is handy; one can tell what one has got.
No need to bargain or to barter first;
Women and wine are there to slake your thirst.
If you want gold, the banker will assign it
And, if he's short, one presently can mine it.
Goblets and lockets are put up for sale;
This paper, once you've paid upon the nail,
Confounds the Thomases who doubt and scoff.
Once form the habit, you can't shake it off.
Thus through the Empire have we guaranteed
Jewels, gold, paper for all future need.

EMPEROR:

To you our realm owes its prosperity;
We will, if we can, reward you fittingly.
To you we entrust the wealth beneath the ground,
In you its best custodians are found;
You know that widespread, well-protected hoard;
To mine it, be it you who give the word.
So now unite, you masters of our treasure,
Fulfil your high and worthy post with pleasure,
In which the underworld, as though in love,
Makes happy union with the world above.

TREASURER:
>Not the least rift will spoil our coalition;
>I'm charmed to have for colleague the magician.

EMPEROR:
>I now reward all persons in my court;
>How they will use it they must make report.

FIRST PAGE:
>I'll live an easy life and have some fun.

SECOND PAGE:
>I'll go and buy my sweetheart chain and locket.

FIRST GENTLEMAN-IN-WAITING:
>I will drink *grand cru* only from now on.

SECOND GENTLEMAN-IN-WAITING:
>The dice already itch me in my pocket.

FIRST KNIGHT:
>My mortgaged land and castle I'll make free.

SECOND KNIGHT:
>It's treasure; it must join my treasury.

EMPEROR:
>I hoped it would inspire you to new actions
>But, knowing you, one guesses your reactions.
>I see it well: for all the wealth in store
>You remain the people that you were before.

FOOL (*entering*):
>Dispensing favours? I need some, I think.

EMPEROR:
>Alive again? You'll spend it all on drink!

FOOL:
>These magic bills! I cannot comprehend them.

EMPEROR:

> That I can well believe; you'll just mis-spend them.

FOOL:

> Still more of them; I don't know what to do.

EMPEROR:

> Just pick them up. I threw them down for you.
>
> (*The Emperor goes out*)

FOOL:

> Five thousand crowns—is that what I've collected?

MEPHISTOPHELES:

> You two-legged wineskin, are you resurrected?

FOOL:

> I've often been—but never quite like this!

MEPHISTOPHELES:

> You're in a sweat, you register such bliss.

FOOL:

> But only look, can I cash this stuff he gave?

MEPHISTOPHELES:

> It will give gullet and stomach all they crave.

FOOL:

> And can I buy a country farm and stock it?

MEPHISTOPHELES:

> Once show that bill, you're never out of pocket.

FOOL:

> And a wooded estate with hunting and fishing?

MEPHISTOPHELES:

> Zounds!
> I'd like to see your lordship ride to hounds.

FOOL:
>   I'll be a squire ere night—I'll show them how!

>   *(He goes out)*

MEPHISTOPHELES (*alone*):
>   Well, well, who says our fool is foolish now?

A DARK CORRIDOR

MEPHISTOPHELES:

> Why lead me through these gloomy galleries?
> Is there not fun enough at court,
> Amidst the dense and coloured throng
> A chance for trickery and sport?

FAUST:

> No more of that; that is a line which you
> Have long worn out like an old shoe;
> But now your dodgings forth and back
> Serve but to throw me off my tack.
> I am tormented what to do;
> The steward presses me, the chamberlain too.
> The Emperor wishes—and one can't ignore him—
> To have Helen of Troy and Paris brought before him,
> To see, produced in their true shapes again,
> The paragon of women and of men.
> So to the work! I dare not break my word.

MEPHISTOPHELES:

> To make this careless promise was absurd.

FAUST:

> You did not realize, my friend,
> Quite what that technique you use meant;
> First, we gave the Emperor wealth,
> Now we must provide amusement.

MEPHISTOPHELES:

> No sooner said than done, you think;
> You stand upon a steeper brink,
> You probe into the strangest realm,
> Increase your debts in the end, it isn't funny,

If you think Helen can be summoned
As simply as that spectral money.
I can supply a cretinous witch, I boast
A line in goitrous gnome and gossamer ghost,
But devils' darlings—while it's no misnomer,
That name—can't pass for heroines out of Homer.

FAUST:

Ah, there we have again your old lament!
You always land one in uncertainties,
You are the father of all hindrances,
Want new rewards for each expedient.
Some mumbo-jumbo and the job is done—
A wink of an eye and there are Paris and Helen.

MEPHISTOPHELES:

The heathen are a race I shun,
They have their private hell to dwell in;
There *is* a means, though.

FAUST:

Tell me! Instantly!

MEPHISTOPHELES:

I'm loath to reveal this lofty mystery.
Goddesses throned in solitude, sublime,
Set in no place, still less in any time—
Even to speak of them embarrasses me.
I mean the Mothers!

FAUST (*startled*):

Mothers!

MEPHISTOPHELES:

You show fear?

FAUST:

The Mothers! Mothers! It's so strange to hear.

MEPHISTOPHELES:

> And strange they are: these goddesses—the same
> To earth unknown whom Hell is loath to name.
> To find them you must plumb the cosmic vault;
> That we have need of them is your own fault.

FAUST:

> Where is the way?

MEPHISTOPHELES:

> No way! To the unvisited,
> Not to be visited; to the unsolicited,
> And not to be solicited. Ready? Yes?
> You will find neither lock nor bolt to bound you,
> But lonelinesses will surround and hound you.
> Can you conceive such desolate loneliness?

FAUST:

> You might have spared me that address;
> This has a smack of the witches' kitchen
> And of a time long since gone by.
> Did I not have to deal with the world
> And learn and teach its vacancy?
> And when my reason voiced my true conviction,
> There rang out doubly loud the contradiction;
> And faced with hideous pranks was forced—no less—
> To fly to solitude, to the wilderness,
> And to live alone, yet not without a friend,
> Had to sell myself to the devil in the end.

MEPHISTOPHELES:

> Suppose that you had swum across the ocean
> And there beheld the limitless,
> There you would see wave after wave in motion;
> Yes, even when afraid the world would cease,
> You'd still see something—you would probably
> See dolphins glancing through the calm green sea;
> See sun and moon and stars and the clouds moving;
> In that ever empty farness you see nothing,
> The step you make you will not hear,
> And where you stand, no ground is there.

FAUST:

> You speak like the first of all the mystagogues
> Who lead their true disciples to the dogs;
> But in reverse. You send me to emptiness
> That there my arts and powers may both increase;
> You treat me like the cat in the tale, require
> That *I* should claw out chestnuts from the fire.
> So be it! We will fathom it or fall,
> And in your Nothing may I find the All!

MEPHISTOPHELES:

> Congratulations, before you part from me!
> You know the devil, that is clear to see.
> Here, take this key.

FAUST:

> That little thing! But why?

MEPHISTOPHELES:

> First seize it; it is nothing to decry.

FAUST:

> It grows within my hand! A glow! A spark!

MEPHISTOPHELES:

> Ah, now you see: a possession worth remark!
> It will find out the place among all others;
> Follow it down, it leads you to the Mothers!

FAUST:

> The Mothers! Again this blow upon my ear!
> What is this word that I so dread to hear?

MEPHISTOPHELES:

> A new word troubles you? Is your scope no more?
> Will you only hear what you have heard before?
> Never again be troubled by such sounds;
> You have long been used to things that pass all bounds.

FAUST:

> My welfare rests upon no rigid plan,
> To feel appalled is the greatest gift of man;

Whatever the world impose as penalty,
His core is moved to feel immensity.

MEPHISTOPHELES:

Sink down then! I could also say, ascend!
It's all the same. Flee from created things
Into the realms of forms no lives attend!
Delight in what have long since not been there;
Their energy twines itself like drifting clouds
But swing the key—keep them away—take care!

FAUST:

Good! Gripping this I feel new strength awaking;
My breast expands, fired for this undertaking!

MEPHISTOPHELES:

A glowing tripod tells you in the end
You have descended whence no souls descend.
There shall you see the Mothers by its light,
Some of whom sit, some walk, some stand upright,
As may occur. Formation, transformation,
Eternal Mind's eternal conservation.
Wreathed with all floating forms of what may be
They see you not, shadows are all they see.
Then pluck up heart, the danger is so great,
Approach that tripod, do not hesitate,
And touch it with the key.

(Faust assumes a commanding attitude with the key)

MEPHISTOPHELES:

                        That's right. A true
Servant, the tripod then will follow you.
Fortune will help you climb, you calmly rise,
Are back—before they notice—with your prize.
And once you have brought it here, brought it to light,
You call that heroic pair out of the night,
The first who had the nerve the venture needed;
Now it is done and you—you have succeeded.
Henceforward, as magic custom has bespoke,
Gods must appear out of that incense smoke.

FAUST:

What now?

MEPHISTOPHELES:

Now let your being downward strive;
Stamp and you sink. Stamp, you'll return alive.

(Faust stamps and sinks out of sight)

Will the key prove perfect? That's the chief concern.
I am curious to know if he'll return.

BRIGHTLY LIT HALLS

(The whole Court in commotion)

COMMANDER-IN-CHIEF:

> You owe us still the spectacle of the ghosts;
> The Emperor's waiting—Implement your boasts!

STEWARD:

> He is just asking for this presentation;
> Don't shame His Majesty by procrastination.

MEPHISTOPHELES:

> But that is why my crony has departed;
> He has been well briefed how to start it,
> And has to make most special efforts
> Locked away quietly; the fact is
> The man who has to raise this prize of beauty
> Requires the highest art which wizards practise.

STEWARD:

> What arts you use is an irrelevance;
> The Emperor wants the show to start at once.

BLONDE *(to Mephistopheles)*:

> A word, sir. You observe my clear complexion;
> In the nasty summer it won't bear inspection.
> Hundreds of brownish freckles come out then
> To my disgust all over my white skin.
> A cure!

MEPHISTOPHELES:

> A pity! Such a glowing jewel
> To get spots in May like your leopard cub, it's cruel.

Take frogs' spawn, toads' tongues, mix well with a spoon,
Duly distil by the light of the full moon,
And, when it wanes, apply it undiluted—
Comes the Spring, your spots will be uprooted.

BRUNETTE:

The crowd press round to get in your good graces.
I have a frozen foot—I crave a cure!
It hinders me when I try to show my paces
And makes even my curtseying unsure.

MEPHISTOPHELES:

Permit a stamp of my foot upon your own.

BRUNETTE:

That usually suggests some amorous leaning—

MEPHISTOPHELES:

Child, when I do it, there's a deeper meaning.
Homoeopathy will cure each part concerned;
Foot heals foot and so with every member.
So watch! I'll stamp! It will not be returned.

BRUNETTE (*screaming*):

Oh! Oh! It burns! So hard a stamp, to be sure,
It was like a hoof.

MEPHISTOPHELES:

Oh, that's just part of the cure.
Now you can dance your fill, you will discover;
Go, foot it under the table with your lover.

LADY:

Let me get through! My sorrows are too great,
They burrow and boil in my heart and won't abate;
Till yesterday he sought happiness in my sight,
To-day he flirts with *her*, ignores me quite.

MEPHISTOPHELES:

> A serious case but listen to what I say.
> You must press up to him softly for a start,
> Then take this piece of charcoal, daub a dab
> On his sleeve, his cloak, his shoulders, where you may;
> And gracious penitence will prick his heart.
> You must swallow the coal at once to set things right,
> And let your lips touch neither wine nor water;
> You'll have him moaning at your door to-night.

LADY:

> Not poison, is it?

MEPHISTOPHELES (*annoyed*):

> Give it due respect!
> To find such charcoal you must travel far.
> It comes from a pyre that formerly
> We stirred and fanned with more effect.

PAGE:

> I am in love, they say I am too young.

MEPHISTOPHELES:

> (*aside*) I no longer know whom to answer in this throng.

MEPHISTOPHELES:

> (*to Page*) The youngest girl, don't pin your hopes on *her*;
> Those more advanced will think you worthier.

> (*Others come pressing up to him*)

> More clients still! Fighting with fist and tooth!
> I must in the end fall back upon the truth;
> The worst expedient. But I'm troubled so.
> O Mothers, Mothers! Only let Faust go!

> (*He looks around*)

> Already the lights in this hall are burning low,
> As the whole court begins to rise and go.
> I see them move in file and decorously
> Down each long passage, distant gallery.

And now! They are gathering in the ancient Hall
Of the Knights, so vast—and yet it seems too small.
On each wide wall a tapestry tells its tale,
Corner and niche are hung with coats of mail.
There's no need here, I think, for a magic word;
A ghost would find this place of its own accord.

THE HALL OF THE KNIGHTS

(Dim illumination)

HERALD:

Though long the announcer at this theatre,
The secret rule of the spirits baffles me;
In vain one ventures upon rational grounds
To analyse their confused authority.
Chairs and stools are ready for the audience;
The Emperor's seat is just before the stage,
Where he can see with the maximum of comfort
The tapestried battles of the Heroic Age.
He and his lords, now each is in his seat,
The benches in the background are replete;
And lovers too at this dark spirit-tide
Find room for their beloveds at their side.
So, now that all are duly settled here,
We all are ready; let the ghosts appear!

(Trumpets)

ASTROLOGER:

Let the play begin at once; do not despise
The Emperor's orders; let the curtain rise!
Delays are over, magic is on hire,
The curtain disappears as furled by fire;
The wall divides, folds back, there appears to come
Rising up out of nowhere a deep stage
To bathe us all in a mysterious light—
And I myself mount the proscenium.

MEPHISTOPHELES *(emerging in the prompter's box)*:

As prompter all, I trust, will find me slick,
Since promptings are the devil's rhetoric.

ASTROLOGER:

> Before our eyes appears through sorcery
> An ancient temple, massive as can be.
> Like Atlas shouldering heaven long ago
> Here stand its many columns, row on row;
> And well they might suffice that weight of rock,
> Two of them could support a city block.

ARCHITECT:

> You call that classical! I couldn't praise it;
> Heavy and burdensome is how I'd phrase it.
> The coarse and clumsy they call great and solemn.
> I love the boundless urge of the slender column;
> The pointed arch raises the soul on high;
> Such edifices most can edify.

ASTROLOGER:

> Welcome with reverence the star-favoured hours;
> Let reason be subdued by magic powers;
> On the other hand grant a fair course and free
> To exalted and audacious fantasy.
> What you boldly wish, let now your eyes receive it:
> Impossible—which is why one must believe it.

> *(Faust appears on the other side of the proscenium)*

ASTROLOGER:

> In priestly robes and wreath a miracle-man
> Will now fulfil what he in hopes began.
> And with him from the crypt a tripod rises;
> That censer will soon function, one surmises.
> He prepares himself this lofty work to bless;
> Henceforward look for nothing but success.

FAUST:

> In your name, Mothers, each upon your throne
> In the infinite, eternally alone
> And yet in company! Around you weave
> The forms of life, which move but do not live.
> What once existed in full glow and flame,
> It still moves there, eternity its aim.

And you, omnipotent Powers, apportion it
To the tent of day or to the vault of night.
And some are caught up in life's kindly wheel,
Others the wizard seeks with nerves of steel,
And confidently lavishes what all
Desire—to see a miracle befall.

ASTROLOGER:

The glowing key has barely touched the censer
And the place is wrapped in a vapour, denser, denser,
Which filters in and like a cloud comes gliding,
Stretched out, massed, interlaced, pairing, dividing.
And now observe a phantom masterpiece!
The clouds make music as they curve and crease.
From airy tones wells up a mystery
And, while they move, all turns to melody.
The shaft of the pillar like the triglyph rings,
I believe indeed that the whole temple sings.
Now the mist drops and from the veils it shed
There steps a comely youth with a dancer's tread.
Here ends my task, I have no need to name him—
The charming Paris, who would not acclaim him?

(Paris steps forward)

LADY:

O what a glow and strength of blooming youth!

A SECOND:

Just like a fresh and juicy peach, in truth!

A THIRD:

Such finely drawn and sweetly swollen lips!

A FOURTH:

At such a cup *you* might be one who sips.

A FIFTH:

He's very pretty, though not quite refined.

A SIXTH:

    He could be a shade more polished to my mind.

KNIGHT:

    I think I detect the shepherd in his face
    But of the prince and court—no, not a trace.

ANOTHER:

    But he's half naked, he really is, the charmer;
    To judge, we'd have to see him first in armour.

LADY:

    He sits down, languorously, pleasantly.

KNIGHT:

    You might be comfortable on his knee.

ANOTHER:

    He droops his arm so daintily over his head.

GENTLEMAN-IN-WAITING:

    The boor! I would call that prohibited.

LADY:

    You gentlemen can pick holes in everyone.

GENTLEMAN-IN-WAITING:

    To loll in the Emperor's presence, that's not done.

LADY:

    He's on the stage. He thinks he's quite alone.

GENTLEMAN-IN-WAITING:

    Even the drama should respect the throne.

LADY:

    The dear boy's overcome, he's gently sleeping.

GENTLEMAN-IN-WAITING:

    He'll be snoring next. Naturally. It's in keeping.

YOUNG LADY (*enchanted*):

> Mixed with the incense what is that sweet scent
> That gives my inmost heart cool nourishment?

OLDER LADY:

> Ah yes! Deep in my soul a breath is blowing,
> It comes from him!

OLDEST LADY:

> It is the bloom of growing,
> Which like ambrosia in this youth is found
> Prepared to spread its aura far around.

(*Helen steps forward*)

MEPHISTOPHELES:

> So that is Helen! I should lose no sleep
> For her; she's pretty but she's not my type.

ASTROLOGER:

> For further words from me there's no more need;
> That, as a gentleman, I must concede.
> The beauty comes and had I tongues of fire—
> Beauty has always tuned the poet's lyre;
> To whom she appears, he suffers ecstasy;
> To whom she belonged, too fortunate was he.

FAUST:

> Have I still eyes? Deep in my consciousness
> Does the spring of beauty pour her vast largesse?
> My quest of terror brings a blissful prize.
> How null and shuttered the world was to my eyes!
> What is it now since I became a priest?
> Miraculous, durable, securely based.
> Let the breath that gives me life expire if I
> Ever lapse back from you and my new duty!
> The lovely form that once enraptured me,
> That blest mirage of sorcery,
> Was a mere foam-draft of such beauty.
> It is you to whom all powers that stir in me,
> Sum of my passion, my propensity,
> Love, adoration, frenzy, are tribute due.

MEPHISTOPHELES (*from the box*):
> Collect yourself; that rôle is not for you.

OLDER LADY:
> Fair size, good figure, but her head's too small.

YOUNGER LADY:
> Just look at that lumpish foot! Won't pass at all!

DIPLOMAT:
> I have seen duchesses of just this kind;
> From head to foot she's lovely, to my mind.

COURTIER:
> She draws near to the sleeper, soft and sly.

LADY:
> So plain beside that youthful purity!

POET:
> It is reflected beauty on his part.

LADY:
> Endymion and Luna! As in art!

POET:
> Quite right! The goddess seems to droop and sink,
> She bends as though his breath were hers to drink;
> Oh enviable! A kiss! His cup is full!

DUENNA:
> In public! But it's mad! Intolerable!

FAUST:
> Appalling favour for the boy!

MEPHISTOPHELES:
> 　　　　　　Keep still!
> Be quiet! Let the ghost do what she will.

COURTIER:
> She steals away on tiptoe—and he wakes.

Now she looks round. I expected just such tricks.

COURTIER:

He's dazed! It's something marvellous and new.

LADY:

No marvel from the lady's point of view.

COURTIER:

Now she turns round to him with modest grace.

LADY:

I can see she feels he needs to be rehearsed;
All the male sex are fools in such a case,
He really and truly thinks that he's the first.

KNIGHT:

She'll pass with me! Such queenly delicacy!

LADY:

The courtesan! That's just vulgarity!

PAGE:

I'd like to be in Paris' shoes, you bet!

COURTIER:

Who would not be a fish in such a net?

LADY:

The trinket has been passed around enough,
I think the gilt is pretty well worn off.

ANOTHER:

Since she was ten she's been a good-for-nothing.

KNIGHT:

At times we all accept the best in view;
I'd cling to such a lovely residue.

PEDANT:

> I see her certainly but my mind must out:
> If she's the real Helen one may doubt.
> The evidence of one's eyes is most misleading,
> I base my judgments mainly on my reading.
> Which tells me how that real Helen of Troy
> Inspired the greybeards with peculiar joy;
> In my opinion, this fits perfectly:
> I am not young, yet she gives joy to me.

ASTROLOGER:

> No more a boy! A daring hero now,
> He embraces her—which she must needs allow.
> He lifts her up in arms that over-rule,
> Will he really bear her off?

FAUST:

> Presumptuous fool!
> D'you dare? Are you deaf? This is too much! Stop!
> Stay!

MEPHISTOPHELES:

> But you yourself put on this phantom-play.

ASTROLOGER:

> Only one word! What there remains to tell in
> This piece requires the name: The Rape of Helen.

FAUST:

> The rape! I am here still, do I count for nothing?
> This magic key, is it not in my hand?
> Which led me through wastes and waves, through fright
>   and frothing,
> Through lonelinesses here to this firm strand.
> Here is sure ground! Realities are here,
> Here spirit dare strive with spirits, and prepare
> For itself a double realm, wide as the air.
> Far though she was, how could she nearer be?
> I save her—and she twice belongs to me.
> I'll venture! Mothers! You Mothers! Grant it so!
> The man who has known her cannot let her go.

ASTROLOGER:

> Faust! What are you doing? Look at him!
> He clasps her strongly—and her form grows dim.
> He turns the key towards Paris, he marches on,
> He touches him! Oh! Going! Going! Gone!

(Explosion. Faust lies on the earth. The spirits dissolve in mist)

MEPHISTOPHELES (*hoisting Faust on his shoulders*):

> That's that. To burden oneself with fools, you see,
> In the end does even the devil injury.

(Darkness. Tumult)

ACT II

*

HIGH-VAULTED, NARROW GOTHIC CHAMBER, FORMERLY FAUST'S, UNALTERED

(Mephistopheles enters from behind a curtain. While he holds it up and looks behind him, one sees Faust stretched out unconscious on a superannuated bed)

MEPHISTOPHELES:
>Lie here, unhappy! Led astray
>Into the nets which bind a lover!
>Whom Helen paralyses, he
>Cannot so easily recover.
>I look aloft, across and back . . .
>Unchanged, intact, on every side;
>Though the stained glass is dustier, I think,
>The spiders' webs have multiplied;
>The ink is dry, the paper has gone yellow;
>Yet everything remains in place—
>Even this quill which Faust once used
>To sell himself to the devil and forfeit grace.
>Yes—and sunk deeper in its stem
>The little drop of blood I coaxed from him.
>The greatest connoisseur I know—
>I'd wish him luck with such a curio.
>And here his old gown hangs on the same old hook;
>I really feel a disposition,
>You smoke-warmed garment, donning you
>To venture forth as a man of erudition
>And don infallibility too—
>A feat among professors, though
>The devil outgrew it long ago.

(He shakes the fur. Crickets, beetles and moths fly out)

CHORUS OF INSECTS:
>Welcome [O welcome],
>>Patron and doyen!
>We come and we hum and
>>We know you again.
>You planted us singly
>>Where none could discern;
>But dancing in thousands
>>Papa, we return!
>The knave in the bosom
>>Lies low like a fraud
>But the lice in the sheepskin
>>Come gladly abroad.

MEPHISTOPHELES:
>Surprising how this young creation takes my mind!
>Just sow them—and you'll reap a crop, you'll find.
>Now one more shake to this old furry clout—
>And still some here and there come fluttering out.
>Up and around, my sweethearts! How you hover
>And race for a thousand corners to take cover!
>There where the ancient cases stand,
>Here in a parchment time has tanned,
>In ancient potsherds, dusty, dull,
>And in the eye-holes of each skull.
>Such a mildew, such a mess,
>Gives endless scope for whimfulness.
>Come, cloak my shoulders, musty fur!
>To-day I am Vice-Chancellor.
>Though the title is futility.
>Where are the people to acknowledge me?

(He pulls the bell which gives out such a penetrating sound that the halls tremble and the doors spring open)

FAMULUS (*staggering down the long dark passage*):
>What a clanging! What a quaking!
>Stairs are swaying! Walls are shaking!
>Through the coloured panes that tremble
>See the thunder storm assemble!

Jumps the floor and from the ceiling
Rains the plaster, parting, peeling.
And the door, with bolt and bar,
Magic powers have thrown ajar.
Look! How terrible! A giant
Stands in Faust's old gown, defiant!
As he stares and beckons me
I feel a giving at the knee.
Shall I fly? Or shall I stay?
Oh, what must I expect to-day!

MEPHISTOPHELES (*beckoning*):
Come in, my friend. Your name is Nicodemus.

FAMULUS:
Respected sir! That is my name—*Oremus*.

MEPHISTOPHELES:
That we'll omit.

FAMULUS:
You know me; I'm so glad.

MEPHISTOPHELES:
I do indeed: a student though no lad,
My moss-grown friend! A learned man like you
Sticks to his desk—he's nothing else to do.
A moderate house of cards, the greatest wit
Who starts to build it cannot finish it.
Your noble master, though, *he* knows the game—
Your Doctor Wagner, he of world-wide fame,
In the academic world he's now the ace;
It's he alone who holds that world in place,
He—wisdom's daily propagator.
And audiences wanting all the data
Cluster around him thick as clover;
He shines uniquely ex cathedra,
He wields a key just like St. Peter,
Unlocks the Under and the Over.
No name nor fame can now withstand him,

He glows and sparkles at the centre,
Even the name of Faust is darkened
And Wagner is your sole inventor.

FAMULUS:

Excuse me, honoured sir, if I've the face
To tell you that is not the case
And all such thoughts are out of place
Since modesty is Wagner's modest part.
The inexplicable disappearance
Of that great man affects his mind's coherence;
He prays that Faust return to clear and cheer his heart.
This room, just as in Dr. Faustus' day,
Untouched since he went far away,
Awaits its old proprietor.
I hardly dare to enter, sir.
But what are the fateful stars about?
The very walls, I thought, showed fear;
The doorposts shook, the bolts sprang out,
Or *you* could not have come in here.

MEPHISTOPHELES:

Where has your master vanished to?
Take me to him—or fetch him you.

FAMULUS:

His interdict is so severe
I really don't know if I dare.
His great work keeps him on a diet,
For months, of quintessential quiet.
The daintiest of men of learning
You'd think his job was charcoal-burning,
Black in the cheek and red in the eye
From fanning fires of alchemy;
Thirsting for every moment—clang—
His tongs make music as they bang.

WAGNER'S LABORATORY

WAGNER:

The bell rang out—appallingly;
These sooty walls felt the vibration.
No longer can uncertainty
Protract my tensest expectation.
Already the darknesses are clearing;
And in the phial's heart already
Like a live coal it's burning steady;
Like a priceless ruby see it spark
And fork like lightning through the dark.
A pure white light extends, portends!
Oh not to lose it as before!
Ah God, what's rattling at the door?

MEPHISTOPHELES (*entering*):

Welcome, dear sir! We come as friends.

WAGNER:

Welcome to the hour fore-cast!
But guard your life, let word nor breath come past,
I have all but ended my great undertaking.

MEPHISTOPHELES:

What is it then?

WAGNER:

A man is in the making.

MEPHISTOPHELES:

A man? And what enamoured couple
Have you got locked up in your furnace?

WAGNER:

God forbid! We declare all that a farce,
That common mode of him-and-herness.

The tender point from which life sprang at first,
The gracious power which pressed within and burst
And took and gave, destined to shape its throne
And make the near and then the far its own,
That power is now dethroned from high employment;
A beast may still find that it gives enjoyment
But man with his great gifts must now begin
To look for a higher, higher origin.

(*He turns to the fire*)

See how it glows! Now really there's a chance
That the myriad ingredients
Which we have mixed—the mixture is the feat—
Of human stuff by gradual synthesis
In an alembic such as this
Subdued to due catalysis
May quietly make the experiment complete.

(*He turns again to the fire*)

The stuff evolves! More clearly moving—
Conviction stronger, stronger proving:
The mystery that in nature earned one's praise
We dare essay by rational incubation,
And what *she* managed in organic ways
We bring about by crystallization.

MEPHISTOPHELES:
A man of years and much experience
No novelty on earth can make surprised.
I also in my wander-years have seen
Plenty of human beings crystallized.

WAGNER (*attending to the phial*):
It rises, flashes, will concrete—
A moment and the work's complete.
A great resolve seems crazy at the start
But chance will give us cause for laughter later:
A brain that can think perfectly will also
Later have a thinker for creator.

(*He gazes at the phial in rapture*)

The glass rings out through some endearing power,
It clouds, it clears; the climax must arrive!
I see a charming little man
In dainty outlines come alive.
What can we now, what can the world ask more?
The mystery lies within our reach.
Just listen to this tenuous sound
Becoming voice, becoming speech.

HOMUNCULUS (*speaking from the phial to Wagner*):
Well, Dad! How are you? That was not a jest.
Come, clasp me in all tenderness to your breast!
But not too tightly—do not break the glass.
That is the way things are, alas:
The cosmos hardly serves the natural kind,
The artificial needs to be confined.
(*to Mephistopheles*) But you, sir, are you here, my cousin Pranks,
At the right moment? Please accept my thanks.
A good chance brings you to our company;
While I exist I must show energy.
I'd like to gird myself for work this minute.
You have the skill to help me to begin it.

WAGNER:
Just one word first. Till now, when I was harassed
By old and young with problems, I was embarrassed.
For instance: nobody could grasp precisely
How soul and body are conjoined so nicely
In such a bond as nothing could dissever—
And yet they spoil each other's days for ever.
And furthermore—

MEPHISTOPHELES:
Hold on! *I'd* ask more gladly
Why man and woman get along so badly.
Start on this course, my friend, you'll find no land.
Our little man wants work—here's work on hand.

HOMUNCULUS:
What is on hand?

MEPHISTOPHELES (*pointing to the side door*):
>   Come! Show your talents here!

WAGNER:
>   You are the loveliest little boy, I swear!

> (*The side door opens and Faust is seen on his bed*)

HOMUNCULUS (*astonished*):
>   Significant!

> (*The phial slips out of Wagner's hands and hovers over Faust,
> throwing a light on him*)

>   Surrounded with fair dreams!
> Clear waters in a grove . . . and girls undressing,
> The fairest of the fair . . . better and better . . .
> But one shines out in loveliness surpassing,
> Born of the highest heroic or godly line.
> She dips her foot in the transparent brilliance;
> Her queenly body's charm and flame of life
> Cools itself in the crystal wave's resilience.
> But oh, what whirr is this of swift wings crashing
> Into the placid mirror, rushing, plashing?
> The girls take fright and run away; the queen
> Remains, however, gazing, still serene
> And with a proud and feminine joy she sees
> The prince of swans come nestling to her knees,
> Thrustfully tame. . . . As making soft advances.
> But at once there rises up a close-knit pall
> Of mist and hides that scene of all,
> That scene of all which most entrances.

MEPHISTOPHELES:
>   For what a far-fetched tale you have to answer.
>   A little fellow but a big romancer.
>   I can see nothing—

HOMUNCULUS:
>   Granted. *You*, brought forth
> And reared in the Fog Age of the North

In a mush of chivalry, popery,
How could *you* have eyes to see?
You're at home in obscurity.

(*He looks around*)

Blackened stones, mouldy, obscene,
Gothic and crocketed and mean!
And, once Faust wakes, new troubles lie ahead:
He will stay here for ever—dead.
Wood fountains, swans and naked beauties,
Such was the way his dreaming ran;
How could he endure this place!
All my pliancy scarcely can.
Now take him hence—

MEPHISTOPHELES:

But where? This is entrancing.

HOMUNCULUS:

Command the warrior to the fight
Or lead the maiden to the dancing—
At once they find their heart's delight.
I have just thought, it's even now
The Classical Walpurgis Night—
The very happiest accident.
Bring Faust to his own element!

MEPHISTOPHELES:

The Classical what? I've never heard of it.

HOMUNCULUS:

How could *your* ears have even caught a word of it?
Romantic phantoms only are known to you;
A genuine phantom must be classic too.

MEPHISTOPHELES:

All right—but what's your goal? That is the question.
My hellenic colleagues give me indigestion.

HOMUNCULUS:

>North-westward, Satan, lies your pleasure-ground;
>To-day it is south-eastward we are bound.
>Through a great plain Peneios freely takes
>His bush-bound, tree-bound course through quiet lakes;
>Only the mountain glens confine the view,
>Above which there lies Pharsalus—old and new.

MEPHISTOPHELES:

>Oh! Cut it out! You can ignore for me
>Those broils of tyranny and slavery!
>It bores me; for their war is hardly done
>Before another war must be begun;
>And no one sees himself a marionette
>Who's teased by Asmodaeus behind the set.
>They say they're fighting for the rights of freedom—
>Slave against slave, should you more truly heed 'em.

HOMUNCULUS:

>Men are perverse. Leave them to dree their weird;
>Each must defend himself as best he can
>From boyhood—so at last become a man.
>The question here is how can Faust be cured.
>If you've a method, try it instantly;
>But, if you cannot, leave the task to me.

MEPHISTOPHELES:

>I could essay many a Brocken-stunt
>But heathendom seems barred on every front.
>The Greeks were never up to much! They daze you
>With licensed sensuality which betrays you
>Into committing sins which look like fun—
>Our sins seem gloomy by comparison.
>And now what?

HOMUNCULUS:

>   Well, you're not in general shy;
>And when I tell you of Thessalian witches,
>I have said something, haven't I?

MEPHISTOPHELES:

>Thessalian witches! Really! Those are ladies
>I've long been curious about.
>But to spend nights on nights with them
>Is not all pleasure, I much doubt.
>Still, just to call, to experiment—

HOMUNCULUS:

>Bring here
>The cloak and throw it round our knight!
>The magic cloth, as heretofore,
>Will bear the two of you all right;
>I'll light the way.

WAGNER (*anxiously*):

>And I?

HOMUNCULUS:

>Now, Wagner, *you*—
>You stay, you have most weighty things to do:
>Old parchments to unroll and, as directed,
>The elements of life to be collected
>And mixed with all the care you can apply.
>Consider the What, consider more the How.
>Meanwhile I'll wander through the world a stretch
>And find—who knows—the dot upon the i.
>Then is your great goal won for you;
>Such a reward befits such efforts: wealth,
>Honour and fame, a life of length and health,
>And knowledge—and, it's possible, virtue too.
>Farewell!

WAGNER:

>Farewell! This leaves me broken-hearted.
>I fear we two for evermore are parted.

MEPHISTOPHELES:

>Now to Peneios! Quick! Let's go!
>Do not despise my small relation.
>(*to the audience*) In the end we all depend, you know,
>On creatures of our own creation.

CLASSICAL WALPURGISNIGHT

(The Pharsalian Fields. Darkness)

ERICHTHO:
>To this night's feast of fear, as often in time past,
>I enter now, Erichtho, I the sombre one;
>Not so abhorrent as the obnoxious poets
>Slander and travesty me . . . who never stop
>Praising and blaming. . . . Now I can see the valley
>Blanched far and wide by the waves of ancient tents,
>The afterview of that sorrowful fearful night
>How often already repeated! And to repeat itself
>Always into eternity. Neither will yield his rival
>The empire; and no one yields it to him who got it by
>>force
>And forcefully rules it. For each, though he cannot
>>govern
>His inner self, would only too gladly govern
>His neighbour's will as his own proud mind dictates. . . .
>But here at Pharsalus was fought a master model
>To prove how might opposes greater might and tears
>To shreds the lovely thousand-petalled wreath of freedom
>While the stiff laurel twists around the royal head.
>Here Pompey the Great had dreams of early burgeoning
>>greatness,
>There wakeful Caesar watched the wagging tongue of
>>the balance!
>It is time to measure their strength. And the world knows
>>who won.
>
>The watch-fires glow and spread their red largesse of
>>flames,
>The soil breathes out reflection of shed blood,
>And lured by the rare and marvellous gleam of the night
>The legion of Greek legend keeps its rendezvous.

Round every fire there wanders anxiously or sits
At ease some fabulous figure of ancient time. . . .
The moon, not yet at the full, but shining clear,
Rises and spreads on all a gentle gleam;
The mirage of the tents fades, the fires burn blue.

But above me what is this unexpected meteor?
Alight and lightening the terrestrial ball.
I scent a waft of life. It will not become me
To come near living things, to whom I am harmful;
That brings me ill repute and helps me nothing.
Already it is descending. Prudence! Let me depart.

(*She departs. Enter, above, the air-travellers*)

HOMUNCULUS:

Over fires and fears of horror
One more flight around the circle;
Vale and dale are like a mirror
In which everything is spectral.

MEPHISTOPHELES:

As through some old window showing
Northern chaos, Northern fear,
Here I see repugnant phantoms,
Feel at home, yes, even here.

HOMUNCULUS:

Look! In front! A towering figure
Moves away, with great strides striding.

MEPHISTOPHELES:

Frightened probably to see us
Through the air above her gliding.

HOMUNCULUS:

Let her stride. But Faust, your hero,
Set him down upon the earth—
Life returns at once; this legend
Realm is where he seeks rebirth.

FAUST (*as he touches the ground*):
Where is she?

HOMUNCULUS:

We can't say, I fear;
But, like as not, you'll find out here.
You may in haste, before it dawns,
From flame to flame pursue the trail;
Against the man who dared the Mothers
No further peril can avail.

MEPHISTOPHELES:

I too am in my element here;
And the best course I know for our good cheer
Is that each person through the fires
Seek such adventures as himself requires.
And, as a sign to reunite us,
Let *your* light, little fellow, sound and light us.

HOMUNCULUS:

It will sparkle so—and so 'twill sound.

(*The glass resounds and shines out powerfully*)

Now for new wonders! Outward bound!

FAUST:

Where is she? Ask no more—not now among
These scenes. Without the glebe which bore her,
Without the approaching wave which broke before her,
I still should have the air which spoke her tongue.
Here! Through a miracle, here in Greece! I stood
On her soil and felt at once the soil was good.
And through my sleep a spirit glowed and fanned;
So, tempered like Antaeus, here I stand
And finding here convened the strangest throng
Search through this maze of flames with purpose strong.

(*He goes off on his own*)

ON THE UPPER PENEIOS[1]

(Prelude of Sirens above)

MEPHISTOPHELES:

> Who are these birds the cradling branches
> Conceal beside the poplar stream?

SPHINX:

> Beware of them! This very sing-song
> Has conquered men of most esteem.

SIRENS:

> Ah, those sphinxes—they are odious!
> Why consort with things degrading?
> Hearken, here we come parading,
> Here we sing in tones melodious;
> So we Sirens find it seemly.

SPHINXE *(picking up their tune to mock them)*

> Force them to come down. For riding
> In those branches they are hiding
> Hideous hawk-claws; they'll decoy you,
> Fall upon you and destroy you,
> Should you listen to their song.

SIRENS:

> Away with hate! Away with malice!
> Pour we in the purest chalice
> All the joys beneath the sky!
> On the earth and on the waters
> Making all the gladdest gestures
> That one greets one's dearest by.

[1] The remaining scenes in this Act have been ruthlessly cut.

MEPHISTOPHELES

> Well, these are pretty innovations
> Where throat and strings make permutations
> And braid the notes that flowered apart.
> It's lost on me, such trillful babbling,
> For though my ears must feel their scrabbling
> It does not penetrate my heart.

SPHINX:

> Your heart! Don't mention it. It's futile;
> A leather bottle, shrunk, inutile,
> Would better fit a face so tart.

FAUST (*approaching*):

> How wonderful! I'm glad to see their features—
> Such great strong lines in such repulsive creatures.
> Already I presage a fate that's fair;
> For this grave gaze of theirs will take me—where?
> A sphinx like this saw Oedipus stand in hope;
> Such sirens made Ulysses writhe in rope.
> I feel some new force fill me, thrusting through;
> The forms are great and great the memories too.

MEPHISTOPHELES:

> To-day you seem to relish sights
> Which previously you cursed and banned;
> When a man seeks his love, he'll take
> Even a monster by the hand.

FAUST:

> You sphinxes woman-faced, come, tell me true;
> Helen—has she been seen by one of you?

SPHINXES:

> Helen? Before her day our day was past.
> Hercules killed the last of us, the last.
> But Chiron you could ask, for we forecast
> He canters round upon this spirit-night;
> If you can stop him, you have started right.

SIRENS

May you not once more be cheated!
When Ulysses rode at anchor
Listening to us, free from rancour,
Much he learnt—and could repeat it;
Would you only seek promotion
To our green domains of ocean,
All our wisdom would we give you.

SPHINX:

Let them not, my lord, deceive you!
Whereas Ulysses was self-bound,
Let our good counsel bind you truly:
Find the lofty Chiron duly
And what I promised will be found.

ON THE LOWER PENEIOS

PENEIOS:

    Sway, my rushes with your whispers!
    Gently breathe, bereeded sisters,
    Rustle, willows by my river,
    Lisp, my poplar twigs aquiver,
    Towards my interrupted dream!
    Some frightening premonition wakes me,
    Some strange and vast commotion shakes me
    From my rest, my rippling stream.

FAUST (*coming to the river*):

    If my ears are not deceiving,
    From behind these interleaving
    Arbours, from behind these bushes,
    Comes a sound like human voices.
    Water chattering in fast time,
    Little breezes like—a pastime.

NYMPHS:

    To lie on our margin
    Would suit you the best,
    Revive in our coolness
    The limbs that need rest,
    And find here the peace that
    You never found true;
    We rustle and ripple
    And whisper to you.

FAUST:

    But I'm awake! Oh keep them dominant,
    These lovely forms, these forms pre-eminent,
    Just as my eye projects them there.
    I am transfused so wondrously!
    Are they a dream? A memory?
    Aye, once I had a dream so dear.

The waters sidle through the freshness
Of dense and gently moving bushes,
Not rushing, hardly rippling past,
And from a hundred points a runnel
Converges towards a crystal funnel,
One level spreading bath at last.
The limbs of women young and supple
The liquid mirror proffers double
To the beholder's ravished eye!
And next in bands and gaily bathing,
Boldly swimming, shyly wading,
They splash each other in full cry.
Yes, these should give me glad employment,
My eye in these should find enjoyment,
But ever further yearns my mind.
My glance against that veil thrusts keenly
Where the high queen is hid behind
That tangled foliage bulging greenly.

Now new marvels! Swans are coming,
From their hidden waters swimming,
Moving royally and sleek.
Floating peaceful, fondly pairing,
And yet proud and self-admiring,
How each moves his head and beak!
But one most of all seems vaunting
His audacity and flaunting
Sails through all with eager pace;
Billowing feathers swell and show him
Himself a wave with waves below him,
Pressing towards that hallowed place.
The other swans swim hither, thither,
In all their tranquil sheen of feather,
And soon in splendid strife contend
To distract each timid beauty
That she may forget her duty
And make her safety all her end.

NYMPHS:

Come, my sisters, lay your ear
On the river's grassy roof;

Unless I am deceived, I hear
The thudding of a horse's hoof.
I would I knew what courier might
Be galloping so fast to-night.

FAUST:

The earth appears to boom perforce
Echoing a headlong horse.
    Let me but glance!
    A fortunate chance,
    Shall I achieve it yonder?
    Incomparable wonder!
There gallops up a chevalier,
Seems full of valiance and good cheer,
His horse is white as dazzling snow. . . .
I know him now—no other one—
Philyra's celebrated son!
Stop, Chiron, stop! For what I want to know. . . .

CHIRON:

What? What is it?

FAUST:

    Curb yourself! Go slow!

CHIRON:

I do not rest.

FAUST:

    Then take me with you too.

CHIRON:

Then mount! Now I can make my own inquiry:
Where are you bound for—standing on this bank?
I am prepared to serve you for a ferry—

FAUST (*mounting on his back*):

Where you may choose. I must for ever thank
You, the great man, the noble pedagogue,
Who to his fame brought up an heroic race,
The fair fraternity of the Argonauts
And all who built a world for bards to grace.

CHIRON:

> Leave that; it is irrelevant.
> As mentor even Pallas is low-rated;
> In the end they carry on just in the way they want
> As though they were never educated.

FAUST:

> The leech who gives each plant its name,
> Who knows what powers each root can claim,
> Healing the sick and comforting the sore,
> I embrace him with my body and my core.

CHIRON:

> Heroes who near me suffered hurt
> I could advise and help when younger,
> But in the end I left my art
> To parish priest and simple-monger.

FAUST:

> You are the man who's truly great,
> One single word of praise you hate.
> Modest escape is all you seek
> And make believe you're not unique.

CHIRON:

> Your praise, though feigned, is far from feeble;
> You flatter prince no less than people.

FAUST:

> You must admit, say what you may,
> You saw the greatest heroes of your day,
> You rivalled those who waged the noblest strife,
> A demigod you lived a strenuous life.
> But among all those forms heroical
> Whom did you hold the worthiest of all?

CHIRON:

> In Argo's august complement
> Each man was good according to his bent,
> The power in each man's soul prevailing
> Served him to remedy his fellow's failing.

Castor and Pollux always won the crown
Where youth and beauty weighed the balance down.
Strong will, quick hand, to work their fellows' weal,
Such gifts supplied the Boreads' comely role.
Reflective, powerful, shrewd, of pliant parts,
So stood out Jason, dear to women's hearts.
Orpheus, becalmed in gentle contemplation,
He struck the lyre beyond man's emulation.
Sharp-sighted Lynceus, he by day and night
Brought holy Argo safe through rock and bight.
Courage is only proved in company
Where one man's deeds win general eulogy.

FAUST:

And Hercules? Why not mention him?

CHIRON:

Oh! Do not cause my eyes to swim.
Phoebus I had never seen
Nor Ares, Hermes, and their kind;
But then I saw—and saw it plain—
What all men praise and god-like find.
He was so born to be a king;
A youth, looked royal through and through—
Though subject to his elder brother
And to the loveliest women too.
Earth will not bear his like again
Nor Hebe grant a heavenly throne;
In vain the poet flogs his pen,
In vain the sculptors torture stone.

FAUST:

Let them presume—they never can
Truly portray that conqueror.
You have described the noblest man.
The fairest woman—what of her?

CHIRON:

Ah! Woman's beauty is skin-deep,
Too often a mere frozen form;
My praises only one can reap

Whose life is a fountain glad and warm.
Beauty abides self-blessed and grace
Confers an overwhelming force
Like Helen's, who once rode on me.

FAUST:

You carried *her*! Oh totally
I am lost! But how? But when? But where?
Helen is all I ever wanted.
On what road did you carry her?

CHIRON:

This request is quickly granted.
Castor and Pollux then had just released
Their little sister from a robbers' nest.
The robbers, unaccustomed to defeat,
Soon rallied and came storming in pursuit.
Then the Eleusis marshes blocked our way
And caused the hasting three delay;
The brothers waded, I—I plashed and swam across;
Then she sprang down and stroked the tresses
Of my wet mane and with caresses
Thanked me, so self-aware, so sweetly sage.
How strange her young allure that charmed my age!

FAUST:

Just ten years old!

CHIRON:

             I see, the academicians
Have hoaxed you like themselves with their editions.
A mythical woman is a special case.
Poets present her as she seems in place;
She never grows of age nor old,
Remains enchanting to behold,
Is borne off young, is courted still in age;
Enough, no time can bind the poet's page.

FAUST:

No more let Helen by time's bonds be bound,
Whom even after death Achilles found

Outside all time! What a rare chance, how great,
To wrest one's love out of the hands of fate!
And shall not I, imbued with wild desires,
Draw into life that form the world admires?
That eternal being, born to be divine,
In whom soft grace and height of soul combine?
You saw her once; I saw her even to-day
Fair as alluring, fair as I could pray.
Now is my mind, my being, captured fast;
Unless I win her, I have lived my last.

CHIRON:

Strange man! As human being you are entranced;
Spirits will find it madness far advanced.
But we meet opportunely here;
Just for a little moment every year
I visit Manto the great prophetess,
Whom I most love of all the Sibyl guild,
Not frantic but beneficently mild;
She will succeed—and quickly, be assured—
In making you, by herbs, completely cured.

FAUST:

Cured I refuse to be, my mind is firm;
Would I be like the rest, not man but worm?

CHIRON:

Do not pass by this well of saving grace.
Be quick! Dismount! We have reached the place.
Look up! Behold, portentous, near,
The eternal temple in the moonlight here.

MANTO (*dreaming within*):

Hoofs on the ground!
My temple steps resound.
Demigods their entrance make.

CHIRON:

You are right.
Let your eyes but open! Wake!

MANTO (*waking*):
> Welcome! I see you keep your tryst.

CHIRON:
> Does not your templed home persist!

MANTO:
> Still ever tireless, running riot?

CHIRON:
> Still ever dwelling fenced in quiet,
> While I love circling ceaselessly?

MANTO:
> I wait—and time revolves round me.
> And this man?

CHIRON:
> This notorious night
> Has swirled and washed him to this site.
> 'Tis Helen that with frenzied heart,
> Helen that he wants to win,
> But knows not where nor how to start.
> A most deserving patient.

MANTO:
> Dear to me
> The man who woos impossibility!

> (*Chiron is already far away*)

> Step in, bold man, towards joys benign.
> This darksome passage leads to Proserpine,
> Where deep beneath Olympus she
> Grants proscript audience secretly.
> Orpheus—I smuggled *him* in here by art;
> Use *your* chance better. Quick! Take heart!

ON THE UPPER PENEIOS

SIRENS:

> Plunge ye in Peneios' wave!
> There to swim and plash is fitting,
> Raising songs and songs repeating
> Which unhappy people crave.
> Lacking water none is well!
> Let us all our forces hasten
> To the glad Aegean basin
> Where the waves all joys foretell.

MEPHISTOPHELES:

> Look, in this copse nearby there goes
> A light which most discreetly glows.
> How all things work out pat for us!
> It is indeed Homunculus!
> Well, little fellow, whither bound?

HOMUNCULUS:

> From place to place I hover round
> And hanker in the proper sense for birth,
> Being all agog to break my glass apart—
> But what I have so far seen on earth
> Does not encourage me to start.
> Still—don't repeat this, my good creature—
> I'm on the trail of two philosophers.
> I listened and their cry is 'Nature! Nature!'
> I will stick close to these, I take it
> They know of earthly essence—what can make it;
> Thus I in the end might well find out
> The wisest means to bring my birth about.

MEPHISTOPHELES:

> Your birth? Bring it about yourself!
> Where phantoms are in session, there

Is welcome the philosopher;
Who on the spot creates to please his clients
A dozen brand new ghosts of science.
Without mistakes you can't attain to reason.
You would be born? Be born in your own season!

HOMUNCULUS:

Still, good advice is not a thing to flout.

MEPHISTOPHELES:

Go on then! We shall see how it turns out.

(*They separate again*)

ANAXAGORAS (*to Thales*):

Your mind is stiff and will not bow.
What further argument is needed now?

THALES:

The wave will bow to all the winds that play
But from the rugged cliff it holds away.

ANAXAGORAS:

It was volcanic gas produced this cliff.

THALES:

In moisture is the genesis of life.

HOMUNCULUS (*between the two*):

Permit me to attend on this;
I too desire a genesis.

ANAXAGORAS:

Have you, O Thales, ever in one night
Produced from slime a mountain of such height?

THALES:

Never were Nature and her living floods
Confined to day and night and periods.
Each form she fashions with due providence,
Even in great things there's no violence.

ANAXAGORAS:

> But here there was! A fierce Plutonic fire,
> Explosive gases of Aeolia, dire,
> Burst through that ancient crust of level ground
> That a new mountain might at once be found.

THALES:

> Where will this argument lead us in the end?
> There stands your mountain—that is good, my friend.
> Wrangling like this one loses time; it brings
> No gain save leading patient folk on strings.
> But let us go! The feast Aegean
> Expects strange guests, prepares the paean.

THE AEGEAN SEA

(The moon remaining in the zenith. Sirens lying round on the cliffs: fluting and singing)

SIRENS:

> Though Thessalian sorceresses
> Have ere now in night's distresses
> Drawn thee down to impious dark,
> Moon, look calmly from thine arc
> On these trembling waves a-glimmer,
> On this revelry and shimmer,
> Shed thy light on this commotion
> Rising from the breast of ocean.
> Ever ready slaves of thine,
> Luna, kindly on us shine.

NEREIDS AND TRITONS:

> Sing, sing louder, keener sound,
> Make the broad sea echo round,
> Call the folk that there belong!
> Whence we hid in deepest calm
> From the chasm-carving storm
> We are drawn by lovely song.
>
> See how we, exalted, raptured,
> Don the golden chains we've captured,
> Supplementing crown and jewel
> With embroidered belt and bangle—
> All of which ye here purvey.
> Shipwrecked treasures in a tangle
> Ye have sung to us, ye cruel
> Sirens, demons of our bay.

SIRENS:

> Bide thou in thy height,
> Moon, and grant us friendly light,

That the night delay
Nor sunrise end our play!

THALES (*on the shore: to Homunculus*):

Old Nereus? I'd be pleased to pay a call
On him with you—his cave's not far at all—
But he's a hard old nut to crack,
Old pot of grumps, old stickleback.
The crossgrained fellow cannot find
One ounce of good in all mankind.
Yet, since he reads what is to be,
He is respected generally
And honoured as a lofty pundit;
He has helped many people too.

HOMUNCULUS:

Let's knock and see if that is true;
I think my glass and flame will stand it.

NEREUS:

Do I hear human voices at my door?
What sudden fury fills me to the core!
Creatures that making godhead their endeavour
Remain condemned to be themselves for ever.
Entitled from of old to godly rest,
Yet was I forced to benefit the best;
And, now I see the way events surprised 'em,
It's just as if I never had advised 'em.

THALES:

And yet, old Sea-beard, you retain our trust;
Don't drive us hence; you are the sage; be just!
Regard this flame—human enough; well, he
Will follow your advice implicitly.

NEREUS:

Advice! With *men* never a potent factor!
A wise word freezes in a stubborn ear.
However angry actions scold the actor,
People remain as wilful as before.

Paris—I warned him with a father's care
Before his lust caught Helen in a snare.
Upon the Grecian shore he stood there, bold,
And what I saw in spirit I foretold:
Air rank with smoke, and fire-clouds wreath on wreath,
The rafters red, murder and death beneath—
Troy's doomsday, spellbound in the poet's page
And no less dread than famed from age to age.
The shameless youth contemned what age could tell;
He laughed and went his way and Ilium fell—
A giant corpse, after long torment stiff,
Good eating for the birds on Pindus cliff.
Ulysses too, did I not counsel him
Of crafty Circe and of Cyclops grim?
His dallying, his feather-headed crew,
And God knows what! But what good did it do?
Until much buffeted and late and sore
A kind wave cast him on a friendly shore.

THALES:

Though such behaviour give the wise man pain,
The good man will give counsel once again;
A dram of thanks, to make his heart feel good,
Will far outweigh tons of ingratitude.
And our request is not a thing to scorn:
This boy here wishes to be wisely born.

NEREUS:

Don't spoil my rare good humour—rare, it's true!
To-day I've very different things to do.
I have just summoned hither all my daughters,
The Dorides, the graces of the waters.
Neither Olympus nor your soil can bear
A life that moves so sweetly, looks so fair.
They leap, describing the most graceful courses,
From the sea-dragon on to Neptune's horses,
And with the element are so at home,
They even seem to dance upon the foam.
Riding in Venus' rainbow-coloured shell
Comes fairest Galatea here as well,
Who, since the Cyprian left our realms of brine,

In Paphos is regarded as divine.
And so my lovely daughter as her own
Inherits holy place and chariot throne.
Away! A father's joy must shun eclipse;
No hate should pass his heart, no curse his lips.
Away to Proteus! Ask him to relate
How something can be born and change its state.

(He goes off towards the sea)

THALES:

This step has brought us nowhere; if by chance
One does catch Proteus, he dissolves at once;
And should he stay, he tells you in the end
Only what staggers and confounds the mind.
Yet, after all, such counsel's what you need;
Let's go in search of Proteus. Let's proceed.

(They go off)

SIRENS *(above on the rocks)*:

What is that distant motion,
That gliding through the ocean?
As though by wind's contriving
We saw white sails arriving?
So bright for contemplation
Those nymphs' transfiguration!
Climb down—my heart rejoices
To listen to their voices.

THALES:

Where are you, Proteus!

PROTEUS:

(near) Here! . . .
(far) And here!

THALES:

I pardon your old game of far-and-near;
But spare your friends such tantalizing,
I know that you're ventriloquizing.

PROTEUS (*distant*):
> Farewell!

THALES:

> He's very near. Your light! Look sharp!
> He's as inquisitive as a carp;
> And once he keeps his shape the same
> You can decoy him with a flame.

HOMUNCULUS:
> A flame? At once. I will let pass
> Plenty—but not enough to burst my glass.

PROTEUS (*in the form of a giant turtle*):
> So sweetly lovely! What's this light?

THALES (*hiding Homunculus*):
> Fine! But come nearer if you like the sight.
> Don't let a little effort make you vexed;
> Be human, show yourself a biped next.
> You want to see what we've concealed?
> Be it by us dispensed, by us revealed.

PROTEUS (*in his own shape*):
> I see you're up to all the tricks of earth.

THALES:

> Well, changing shape still gives *you* cause for mirth.

> (*He reveals Homunculus*)

PROTEUS (*astonished*):
> A flaming midget! What one's never seen!

THALES:

> He needs advice, he wants an origin.
> He was, as he himself related,
> Most wondrously but only half created;
> Having no lack of intellectual qualities
> But quite devoid of concrete functionalities.
> Till now his glass is all that gives him weight,
> But next he yearns to be incorporate.

PROTEUS:

>True product of a virgin birth!
>Who've come before your time on earth!

THALES (*whispering*):

>From another side I find the matter critical;
>He is, I think, hermaphroditical.

PROTEUS:

>So much the better for him too;
>However he arrives, he'll do.
>But here's no need for cerebration,
>In the wide ocean you must seek creation.
>There in a small way you begin—
>Glad to devour the smallest creatures—
>Then slowly grow through valve and fin
>And thus evolve to higher forms and features.

HOMUNCULUS:

>The breeze here blows so fondlingly—
>A scent as after rain—it pleases me!

PROTEUS:

>I well believe it, dearest child!
>And further on it's far more pleasant;
>On that thin spit the air's so mild
>That none could tell what aura's present.
>And there the cavalcade appears
>Floating our way—it nears and nears—
>Come with me there!

THALES:

>And so will I.

HOMUNCULUS:

>How triple-quick we spirits fly!

PROTEUS:

>Earthly traffic, low or high,
>Is always merely drudgery;

It is waves that more enliven;
I will bear you as a dolphin
To the waters.

(*He changes himself into a dolphin*)

There! I'm he!
Soon your lot will nothing lack,
Now I take you on my back,
Wed you to the eternal sea.

THALES:

Accept that laudable solution,
Start at the start of evolution;
Enlisted in a rapid plan
Proceed by everlasting norms
Through myriads of living forms,
With time enough to reach to man.

(*Homunculus mounts the dolphin*)

PROTEUS:

Come in your soul to waters distant—
Throughout their length and breadth existent
At once you move as suits your taste;
But do not strive for higher orders
For, once you cross the human borders,
That is the end and all is waste.

THALES:

It all depends. It's sometimes a good plan
To be in one's own time an honest man.

PROTEUS:

One of your type presumably!
They have at least longevity.
Those pallid troops of spirits, why,
I saw you with 'em centuries gone by.

SIRENS (*on the rocks*):

See yon cirrus clouds which circle
Round the moon—a girdle bright?
Doves they are and love-enkindled,

With their pinions white as light.
Troop of birds by love elated,
Paphos has despatched them here;
Now our feast is consummated—
Peace and rapture, full and clear.

NEREUS (*joining Thales*):

Wanderers by night might take
This moon-levee for delusion;
Spirits are of different make
And not such the true conclusion.
Doves they are, who fly attendant
On my daughter's moving shell;
Ages past have taught them well
Such a flight, unique, transcendent.

(*Galatea approaches, riding on her shell*)

It's you, Galatea!

GALATEA:

Oh father! What bliss!
Oh linger, my dolphins! I long to see this.

(*But she is swept away again*)

NEREUS:

Already over, they pass over
In oscillation and gyration;
What reck they of my consternation?
Ah, could they take me with them yonder!
And yet one single glimpse can cheer
And last me for another year.

THALES:

Hail! Once more hail!
How I bloom and regale
On beauties' and truths' penetration!
Everything live is water's creation!
Water keeps all things young and vernal!
Ocean, grant us thy rule eternal.
Clouds—were it not for thee sending them,

Nor fertile brooks—expending them,
Rivers—hither and thither bending them,
And streams—not fully tending them,
Then what would be mountains, what plains and earth?
'Tis thou giv'st livingest life its worth.

CHORUS:

Thou giv'st livingest life its birth.

NEREUS:

They turn now, swaying back afar,
Glance to glance they bring no more;
Circling in long concatenations
In honour of our celebrations,
Winds the innumerable host.
But Galatea's throne of shell—
I see it still, I see it well.
It gleams like a star
Through the tangle,
Shines through the throng, a lovely spangle,
And though so far
Shimmers clearly through,
Ever near and true.

HOMUNCULUS:

Among this gracious wetness
Whatever meets my brightness
Is ravishing and fair.

PROTEUS:

Among this vital wetness
Your light has now such brightness,
Its tone is rich and rare.

NEREUS:

What secret unknown, mid the hosts in the night,
Is now to be shown to our wondering sight?
What flames round the shell, at the goddess's feet?
Now flaring up mighty, now lovely, now sweet,
As though it were moved by the pulses of love.

THALES:

> Homunculus! Proteus beguiled him above.
> And these are the signs of desire overriding;
> This anguish of booming—what grief is betiding?
> The bright throne will smash him to pieces, I doubt;
> Now it flames, now it flashes—and pours itself out!

SIRENS:

> Our waves are transfigured! What marvel of fire
> Makes them scintillate thus as they clash and expire?
> So it shines and it shakes and makes everything bright.
> Those bodies, they glow on their course through the
>   night,
> With fire all-encompassing, swirling and spinning;
> Now let Eros be lord, who gave all things beginning!
> > Hail to Ocean! Hail the waves
> > Which this sacred fire enslaves!
> > Hail to Water! Hail to Fire!
> > Hail the daring of desire!

FULL CHORUS:

> > Hail the breezes' gentle blisses!
> > Hail, mysterious abysses!
> > All things here let all adore—
> > And the elements all four!

ACT III

*

FAUST'S CASTLE IN GREECE

(An inner courtyard, surrounded by fantastic medieval buildings. Helen and her chorus of captive Trojan women have just been transported here by Mephistopheles, disguised as Phorkyas)

CHORUS LEADER:
  Headstrong and headlong fools, only too truly women!
  Dependent on the moment, playthings of the weather,
  Of good luck and of bad luck! And neither good nor bad
  Can you ever endure with calm. One of you always violently
  Contradicts her neighbour—to be contradicted in turn;
  Joy or sorrow—your screaming, your laughter, sound the
    same.
  Now silence! Wait and listen to what our mistress,
  High-minded, may resolve on her behalf and ours.

HELEN:
  Where are you, Pythonissa? Whatever your name may be,
  Step forth from the vaulted porch of this sombre castle!
  Maybe you went to find that wonderful hero prince
  To announce my coming, insure me a fair reception?
  If so, receive my thanks and take me quickly to him;
  I wish an end to wandering. Rest is all I wish.

CHORUS LEADER:
  In vain, Queen Helen, you gaze on all sides round you here;
  That hideous form is vanished, maybe she remained
  There in that cloud in which ourselves, I know not how,
  Came here so quickly though we never took one step.
  Maybe again she roams the dubious labyrinth
  Of this fantastic castle, this huge many-in-one,
  Procuring from its lord a lordly welcome for you.

But see, already, above there, stirring already, thronging
The galleries, thronging the windows, and through the portals
Bustling hither and thither—see, what a crowd of servants;
This indicates for us—the guests—a courteous welcome.

CHORUS:

My heart opens up! Oh see over there
With what modest approach, with what lingering steps,
Most beautiful boys descend in discreet
And well-ordered procession!
                But how? Whose command
Has trained and disposed them, so prompt to appear,
This glorious breed of youth in its bloom?
What most to admire? Their delicate walk
Or the curls of the head round the shine of the brow?
Or maybe their cheeks which are red as the peach
And peach-like are brushed by the softness of down?
I would I could bite them—but tremble to try;
We know of a fruit which, monstrous to tell,
Has left the rash mouth full of ashes.
           Ah, but the fairest,
           Here they come now;
           What do they carry?
           Steps for the throne[1]—
           Carpet and throne—
           Curtain and canopy
           Fit for the throne—
           Over and over in folds it
           Falls in a cloud pavilion
           Over Helen's head—
           Helen, already invited,
           Has mounted the sumptuous throne—
           Come then and gravely
           Form in your ranks on
           The steps of the throne—
           Worthy, oh worthy, three times worthy
           Of Helen, let such a reception be blest!

(Faust appears at the head of the staircase, dressed like a medieval knight)

---

[1] This repetition of the word 'throne' is not in the original. I used it for radio effect and have retained it to stiffen the verse.

CHORUS LEADER:

> If on this man the gods have not, as they often do,
> Conferred for a short time only admirable form
> And stately bearing and lovable presence, if these are not
> A short loan only, then on every occasion
> What he begins will succeed, be it in battle of men
> Or be it that minor warfare with fairest women.
> Far preferable indeed is he to many others
> Whom I myself in my time have seen made much of.
> With slowly solemn, reverently leisurely steps
> I see the prince approach. O Queen, turn round!

> *(Faust approaches; beside him is a man in fetters)*

FAUST:

> Instead of most solemn greeting, as was due,
> Instead of respectful welcome I present
> You this my servant, tightly bound in chains,
> Who, failing in his duty, made me fail in mine.
> Lynceus, kneel down before this queen of women
> And make her full confession of your guilt!
> This man, exalted empress, is my watchman
> Ordained to look around from my high tower
> With rare far-sightedness and keenly scan
> Heaven's spaces yonder and the sweeps of earth
> For what may there or here announce itself,
> For what may move from circling hills to vale
> And up to my strong fort, be it waves of cattle,
> Be it maybe a marching army; those we protect,
> These we encounter. But to-day! This lapse!
> You, Helen, come: he gives no word. We fail
> To give that fullest welcome which we owe
> To such an exalted guest. And for this crime
> His life is forfeit, he would lie already
> Bleeding in well-earned death—but you alone
> Must punish or must pardon—as you choose.

HELEN:

> This so high office you confer on me
> As judge, as ruler, even if it were
> Only to test me, as I must presume—
> Yet I, as judge, must do the law's first duty:
> To hear the accused. Lynceus, defend yourself!

LYNCEUS:

Let me kneel and let me gaze,
Let me die or let me live,
Here and now myself I give
To this god-given woman's praise.

Waiting for the morning's rapture,
Eastward spying out her flight,
From the *south* there burst a sun
Like a miracle on my sight.

Southward it was not the hills,
Not the vales my vision held,
Not the vasts of earth and sky—
It was She, the unparalleled.

Though endowed with eyes that pierce
Like the lynx's on the tree,
Now a dark, deep dream came round me
And I had to strive to see.

Where then could I find my bearings?
Barbican? Drawbridge? Parapet?
Mists revolving and dissolving—
And this goddess nears the gate!

Orientating eye and heart
Her gentle glory gluts my mind;
This all-blinding beauty left me—
Me, poor Lynceus—wholly blind.

I forgot the watchman's duty,
The horn that I was sworn to blow;
Threaten to kill me if you will—
Beauty lays all anger low.

HELEN:

The evil which I brought, it is not for me
To punish. What harsh destiny dogs my life
So to befool, oh misery, everywhere
The hearts of men that they neither spare themselves

Nor anything else that is worthy. Robbing now,
Seducing, fighting, ravaging hither and thither,
Half-gods, heroes, gods, and demons too,
They have carried me hither and thither about in a maze.
If I once embroiled the world, I have done so twice;
And now bring threefold, fourfold troubles on.
Remove this innocent prisoner, let him go;
Let no disgrace strike one the gods have fooled.

FAUST:

I am astounded, Queen, that in one glance
I see the archer sure, the prey she struck;
I see the bow which sped the shaft at Lynceus
And wounded him. But arrows following arrows
Strike me. I feel their criss-cross everywhere—
Feathered and whirring through my keep and court.
What am I now? You make my trustiest servants
At one blow rebels and you make my ramparts
Unsure. Now even my army, I fear, must needs
Obey the conquering, never-conquered woman.
What then remains but to transfer to you
Myself and all I wrongly thought was mine?
At your feet let me, as your loyal knight,
Acknowledge you my sovereign, who no sooner
Appeared than she acquired my wealth and throne.

LYNCEUS (*with a chest and followed by men bearing others*):
You see me, Queen; I now return!
The rich man begs one glance to earn,
Gazing on you he feels at once
Both poor as beggar, rich as prince.

What was I once! What am I now?
What can I wish? What do? And how?
My flashing sight—what use is it?
It but rebounds from where you sit.

Out of the East we migrants came,
At once the West went up in flame;
Our long broad masses rolling past—
The first knew nothing of the last.

The first man fell, the second stood,
The third man clutched his shaft of wood;
Each Goth was backed a hundredfold—
And thousands died unmarked, untold.

We surged along, we stormed along,
From land to land our hand was strong;
And where one day I called the roll
The next another robbed and stole.

We looked around—no time to spare—
One grabbed the fairest of the fair,
One grabbed the bull that trod with force—
And all the horses came of course.

But I—I loved to spy around
For what most rare the world has found;
Whatever was another's prize
Was withered grass in Lynceus' eyes.

Thus flying after precious things
My hawklike vision gave me wings,
Through every pocket I could pass
And every chest seemed made of glass.

And mine thereby were heaps of gold
With jewels peerless to behold;
But now the emerald has sole right
To deck your breast with green on white.

Now let there float 'twixt ear and mouth
The pearl from sea-floors of the south;
But rubies are beyond the pale,
Your red cheek makes their lustre fail.

And so these treasures beyond price
I bring them here to Helen's eyes
And at her feet the harvest lay
Of many a blood-stained battle day.

Dragging all these across the floor,
Such iron chests I still have more;
Admit me to your train and I
Will brim your treasuries to the sky.

No sooner did you mount this throne
Than you subdued and made your own
My understanding, wealth and power—
All bowed before your beauty's flower.

I held it all my own and fast,
To you I loose it now at last.
I thought it genuine currency
Which now I see as trumpery.

Vanished is all that I possessed,
Mowed-down and dried-up grass at best.
Oh with one cheering look restore
The total worth it had before.

FAUST:

Quickly remove the burden boldly won,
With no reproach to you but no reward.
Already all is hers, all that the castle
Hides in its womb; to offer special things
Is futile. Go and order all your treasures
In pile on pile. Display the glorious sight
Of splendours yet unseen. Let the treasure vaults
Sparkle like dancing skies, prepare a heaven
Of lifeless life. And, fit for Helen's tread,
In haste let flowery carpets be unrolled—
Carpet on carpet—so that Helen's foot
Falls upon softness and her glance which blinds
All but the gods may find a pomp to match.

LYNCEUS:

My lord's command is light to obey,
His servant finds obedience play;
Both blood and wealth are subject so
To Helen's beauty's overflow.
All the army now is tame,
All the swords are blunt and lame,

Beside the glory of her form
The sun is neither bright nor warm,
Beside the riches of her face
All the world is empty space.

(*He goes out*)

HELEN (*to Faust*):

I wish to speak to you—but mount these steps
And join me here. This other empty place
Calls for its master and secures me mine.

FAUST:

First let me kneel and dedicate my heart
To you, most noble lady; and the hand
Which raises me beside you, let me kiss it.
Confirm me as your consort in your realm
Which knows no bounds, and win yourself in me
A worshipper, servant, guardian all in one!

HELEN:

Such manifold wonders fill my eyes, my ears.
Amazement strikes me, I have many questions.
But one thing I would know: why that man's speech
Sounded so strange to me, strange and yet friendly.
One sound appears to match itself to another
And, when one word is welcomed by the ear,
A second comes and gives it a caress.

FAUST:

If our traditional speech so soon delights you,
Oh then for sure our song will steal your heart,
Sating the deepest wants of ear and sense.
But it is safest if we try at once;
Exchange of speech entices, calls for answer.

HELEN:

Then tell me how I too can learn this art.

FAUST:

Quite easy, it must issue from the heart.
And when your longing overflows in you,
You look around and ask—

HELEN:

> Who feels it too.

FAUST:

> The soul no more looks on nor back from this,
> The present moment only—

HELEN:

> Is our bliss.

FAUST:

> Our treasure, our high prize, our promised land;
> And who confirms our right to it?

HELEN:

> My hand.

CHORUS:

> Who is there could blame our mistress
> If she grant this castle's lord
> Friendly signs of favour?
> Truth to say, all of us here are
> Prisoners as we often have been
> Ever since Troy's ignominious
> Downfall and the fearful
> Labyrinth of our grievous road.
>
> Women, to men's love accustomed,
> It is not for them to choose,
> All their lot is knowing.
> Whether to blond-headed shepherd
> Or perhaps to black-bristled faun,
> As time may bring the occasion,
> Over their rounded bodies
> Women assign to them equal right.
>
> Near and nearer already they sit,
> Leaning against one another,
> Shoulder by shoulder, knee by knee,
> Hand in hand they lull and loll
> Propped on the throne's

Cushioned imperial luxury.
Majesty does not deny itself
Wantonly showing
Before the eyes of the people
Pleasures proper to secrecy.

HELEN:

I feel myself so far and yet so near,
Am only glad to say: 'I am here! Am here!'

FAUST:

I hardly breathe, my speech is crippled, crossed,
It is a dream and time and place are lost.

HELEN

I feel myself lived-out and yet new-grown,
Enwoven with you and true to the unknown.

FAUST:

What makes our rarest destiny do not ask!
To be, though but for a moment, is our task.

(Pause)[1]

Hereby have I, hereby have you succeeded;
Let what is past behind our backs be hurled!
Oh feel yourself the child of highest godhead,
You belong solely to the early world.

No longer shall my keep confine you!
Even yet in youth's eternal flower
Arcadia near to Sparta yields us
Retreat to pass the raptured hour.

Decoyed to dwell in blessed pastures,
You fled to happiest destiny!
Now let our throne become an arbour,
Arcadian be our lot and free!

---

[1] This pause represents a cut—and the flight of Faust and Helen to Arcadia.

FIELDS OF ARCADY

(A shadowy grove beneath a rocky range. Faust and Helen are invisible. The Trojan women lie around, sleeping)

MEPHISTOPHELES *(disguised as Phorkyas)*:
How long these girls have been sleeping I do not know: and whether
They saw in dream what I saw clear defined in flesh,
That too I do not know, devil though I am, disguised.
Therefore I wake these young things; they shall be astonished.
Come forth! Come forth! Be quick, shake loose your hair!
Aye, shake the sleep from your eyes, stop blinking so, and listen!

CHORUS:
Only speak, oh tell us, tell us what so wonderful has happened!
More than glad are we to hear of things we no way can believe in,
Suffering as we do from boredom, gazing on these barren crags.

MEPHISTOPHELES:
Children, you have scarcely scrubbed your eyes of sleep—and bored
    already?
Well then, listen: in these hollows, in these grottoes, in these arbours
Screen and shelter were provided, as for lovers in an idyl,
For our lord and for our lady.

CHORUS:
              What, within there?

MEPHISTOPHELES:
                          Separated
From the world—and I alone was called to do them silent service.
Aye, for there a sudden laughter echoes through the roomy caverns
And I look: from Helen's lap a boy is springing to the man's,
From the father to the mother—oh the fondling and the dandling,
Badinage of foolish love, screams of fun, halloos of pleasure,

Chop and change and deafen me.
Naked, without wings a Cupid, faun without faun's bestial nature,
See him spring on solid earth; but the earth retaliating
Whirls him high into the air and with a second spring, a third,
See—he skims the cavern roof.
In his hand a golden lyre, all of him a small Apollo,
Gleefully he steps to the edge, steps to the precipice; we marvel,
And his parents in their rapture clutch each other to their breasts.
Now that light around his head? Hard to tell what that is, gleaming;
Golden ornament? Or is it flame of an overpowering spirit?
And he moves with such a rhythm, even as a boy proclaims him
Future master of all beauty, through whose body the eternal
Melodies move—and in this fashion you shall hear him, in this
    fashion
You shall see him and shall wonder with a wonder never known.

(Helen, Faust and Euphorion appear)

EUPHORION:

    When you hear my songs of childhood,
    Straight your own blood starts to sing;
    See me leap and dance, my parents,
    Your hearts too within you spring.

HELEN:

    Love, for bliss in human measure,
    Enters as a noble pair,
    But for rapture as in heaven
    Forms a three, so fair and rare.

FAUST:

    Now is all we craved accomplished,
    I am yours and you are mine,
    And we stand so bound together—
    Never may this bond untwine!

CHORUS:

    Many happy years illumined
    Gently by this gentle boy
    Heap themselves upon this couple!
    How their union gives me joy!

EUPHORION:

> Now let me gambol,
> Leaping on high!
> To dare the breezes
> And scale the sky,
> Such passion fires me
> Though still a boy.

FAUST:

> But caution! Caution!
> Not over-daring!
> Lest mortal fall
> Should end your faring,
> And our dear son
> End all our joy!

EUPHORION:

> I mean to linger
> No more on land;
> Leave go my mantle,
> Leave go my hand,
> Leave go my hair!
> They are all my own.

HELEN:

> O think! Bethink you
> Whose child you are!
> That fair achievement—
> If you should mar
> Mine, yours and his,
> What cause to moan!

CHORUS:

> This union, I fear,
> Will be soon o'erthrown.

HELEN AND FAUST:

> Chasten! Oh chasten
> For love of us
> These desires that hasten

Impetuous!
In this quiet country
Adorn the plain.

EUPHORION:

For your sake only
I pause, remain.

(*He winds through the Chorus and draws them into a dance*)

Here I float lightly round
Girls that delight.
Tell me: The melody—
Is it—the movement—right?

HELEN:

Yes, you must so begin;
Now lead the fair ones in
Intricate rows.

FAUST:

Would this were done! For I
Find such tricks ruin my
Spirit's repose.

CHORUS:

Raising your arms in such
Movement entrancing,
Shaking your locks in such
Splendour of dancing,
When on that skimming toe
Over the earth you go,
Forward and backward dance,
Limb after limb advance,
Then is your aim complete,
Child of desire;
All of our hearts on fire
Lie at your feet.

EUPHORION:

Be you so many
Light-footed roes;

Off with you, now I
New games propose;
I am the hunter,
You be the prey.

CHORUS:

If you would catch us
Soon you are sped,
All that we long for
When all is said
Is but to embrace you,
You star of day.

EUPHORION:

No! Through the thickets!
By stock and stone!
A light exertion
No gains condone;
What needs coercion
I prize alone!

HELEN AND FAUST:

But how wilful! But how frantic!
No hope here of curb or border!
Hear that sound like horns romantic
Echoing over wood and valley;
What an uproar! What disorder!

(*The Chorus return, singly, in haste, leaving Euphorion to leap up the crags*)

CHORUS:

Heavenly poesy,
Heavenward mount on high!
Shine out her fairest star
Far and more far and far!
And yet we hear her voice
Ever—and we rejoice
That poets are.

EUPHORION (*from the distance*):

No, I am no child—behold me;
Bearing arms a young man comes;

Leagued with the strong and free and daring,
In spirit he has heard the drums.
Away!
Nor stay
When glory's road with armies hums.

HELEN AND FAUST:

Scarcely called to life and scarcely
Granted to the cheerful day,
From yon dizzy steps you hanker
To be gone the grievous way.
Are then we
No family?
Is our dear bond a dream gone grey?

EUPHORION:

You hear that thundering on the ocean?
Cross-thunders there from glen to glen?
In dust and foam embattled armies,
The tears and pangs of struggling men!
Now this clear
Command I hear:
I must die nor think again.

HELEN, FAUST AND CHORUS:

What a horror! What a nightmare!
Are your orders then to die?

EUPHORION:

Should I look on from a distance
At this bitter war? Not I!

HELEN, FAUST AND CHORUS:

The pride! Oh the peril!
Death in his eyes!

EUPHORION:

Aye! And I spread now
Wings to the skies!

Thither! I must! I must!
Grant me but flight.

(*He casts himself into the air: is borne up a moment by his garments;
his head shines forth, followed by a train of light*)

CHORUS:

Icarus! Icarus!
Day become night!

(*A beautiful youth falls at their feet. But his body vanishes at once
while the aureole rises like a comet to heaven. His clothes, mantle
and lyre remain on the ground*)

HELEN AND FAUST:

Joy is but throned for
Pain to dethrone.

EUPHORION'S VOICE (*from the depths*):

Leave me not, mother,
In darkness alone.

(*A pause. Then the Dirge of the Chorus*)

CHORUS:

Not alone! Where'er your dwelling,
Still, oh still, we claim to know you;
Ah, though *you* make haste from daylight,
Never can our hearts forgo you.
Yet we hardly can lament you,
Envy must our dirge pervade;
Such your gifts—of song and valour—
Fair and great in sun and shade.

Ah, though born to earthly fortune,
High of lineage, framed for power,
Soon, alas, you lost your birthright,
Soon were stripped of fruit and flower.
Piercing eye to scan the world,
Insight that could plumb the heart,
Fire of love in noble ladies,
And a song all songs apart.

But you ran—and none could hold you—
Free into the mindless snare,
Violently you broke with custom,
Broke with law and did not care.
Yet at last the highest venture
Filled your spirit, brave and true,
And you longed to win you glory—
Glory? That was not for you.

Then for whom is it? Sad question;
Fate no clear reply concedes,
When in days of sheer misfortune
One great nation, silent, bleeds.
But strike up new songs and livening,
Stand no more thus bowed, aghast;
Earth engenders songs again
As she has for ages past.

(*The music ceases. Complete silence.*)

HELEN (*to Faust*):

An ancient word proves true, true even alas to me:
That happiness and beauty last not long together.
The bond of life is snapped as is the bond of love.
Lamenting both I now say sorrowful farewell
And cast myself this once and last time in your arms.
Queen of the Underworld, receive my son—and me!

(*She embraces Faust, her body vanishes, her dress and her veil
remain in his arms*)

MEPHISTOPHELES:

Hold fast what here remains to you of Helen:
This robe. Hold fast to it! Already demons
Are tugging at the corners, would be glad
To drag it down to Hades. So hold fast!
This robe, though not the goddess whom you lost,
Is godlike too. Make use of its high virtue
Which none could price, and soar on it aloft!
It will soon bear you over all things common
Into wide skies—while your endurance last.
We two shall meet again, far, far from here.

ACT IV

*

HIGH MOUNTAINS

(Stark and pointed peaks. A cloud approaches, hovers, then settles upon a ledge. It divides and Faust steps forth from it)

FAUST:

Gazing deep down on lonelinesses underneath my feet,
I carefully walk along this mountainous razor edge,
Having let go my car of cloud which, once a robe,
Through clear days bore me softly over land and sea.
Slowly it now dissolves, not quickly scattered, from me.
Now eastward strains that round and rolling mass of cloud
And strains my incredulous eye which marvels after it.
Look, it divides while moving, wavelike, mutable,
Yet means to assume a shape. Yes! For I see it true:
Upon sun-radiant pillows queenly stretched her length,
But of gigantic size, a woman's form divine,
I see it! How, like Juno, Leda, Helen,
In lovely majesty she floats before my eyes!
Ah, but it breaks already! Shapeless, spreading, towering,
It lingers in the East, like dazzling, distant ice-caps,
To image forth the vast meaning of fleeting days.

Yet floating round me a delicate, tenuous wisp of cloud
Upon my breast and brow still cheers me, cool, caressing;
Now lightly it rises and high and higher, though lingeringly
Gathers itself away. Some ravishing mirage
This—of my youthfullest, longest-wanted, highest good?
From the deepest springs of heart my earliest treasures well;
Aurora's love, so light of wing, is tokened here—
That quickly felt, first, scarcely comprehended look
Which, while I held it fast, outshone all precious things.
Like the soul's beauty now that gracious form ascends,

Yet does not melt but climbs the heights of sky and takes
Away with it the best and inmost part of Faust.

(*Mephistopheles arrives, having followed Faust in seven-league boots*)

MEPHISTOPHELES:

>That's what I call my best foot first!
>But tell me where your wits have flown!
>Why did you land among these horrors,
>These evil dreams of yawning stone?

FAUST:

>A mountain mass is nobly dumb to me,
>I ask not how nor why it came to be.
>When Nature formed herself, self-grounded, founded,
>She made this ball of earth compact and rounded,
>In mountain range and gorge she took delight,
>Lining up crag on crag and height on height.

MEPHISTOPHELES:

>What's that to me? Let Nature go her way!
>The devil too—to his credit—had his say.
>But to speak clear at last, as once to Jesu,
>There in our surface world did nothing please you?
>Where measureless distance told your eye that story:
>The kingdoms of the world and all their glory.
>But you, who crave and never spare,
>Did nothing really tempt you there?

FAUST:

>Oh yes! One great wish filled my breast.
>Guess it!

MEPHISTOPHELES:

>   My friend, that's quickly guessed.
>For me, Metropolis! You know those hives,
>Grown out of noisome bourgeois lives:
>Mean winding alleys, steepling garrets,
>Cramped markets, cabbage, onion, carrots,
>And stalls which blow-flies haunt to purloin
>Their greasy feast from joint and sirloin;

There any day for sure, I think,
You'll find activity and stink.
Then the broad squares and streets arterial
Trying so hard to look imperial;
And lastly—for no gate says No—
Suburbia's endless overflow.
And there I'd love the noisy churning
Of coaches going and returning,
The random ant-heap's mad endeavour—
Thus going and returning ever.
And *I* might drive or ride—be sure
I'd always be the cynosure
Of thousands of respectful eyes.

FAUST:

No, that I find a poor solution.
One's glad that people multiply,
And in their way live easily,
And even get educated—why,
That's how one fosters revolution.

MEPHISTOPHELES:

How can one guess at your ambition?
Sublimely bold, it's safe to claim.
Since you have soared so near the moon's position,
Maybe the moon is now your aim?

FAUST:

Not so. No moon. This earthly cirque
Still offers scope for great achievement.
What I shall do shall cause amazement,
I feel empowered for venturous work.

MEPHISTOPHELES:

To win you glory? Oh dear me!
You've been with heroines, one can see.

FAUST:

I wish to rule! I wish to own!
Glory? The action counts alone.

MEPHISTOPHELES:

> Yet poets will be found to story
> And preach posterity your glory—
> New fools inflamed by one now hoary.

FAUST:

> No fear that *you* will catch on fire!
> How should *you* know what men desire?
> Your bitter malice, dour and dire,
> How should *it* know what men require?

MEPHISTOPHELES:

> So be it, as your fancy pleases!
> Confide to me the range of your caprices.

FAUST:

> My eye was drawn, out to the wastes of ocean;
> It bulged on high, a concentrated tower,
> And then deployed and set its waves in motion
> To storm the far-flung levels of the shore.
> And that annoyed me; just as arrogance
> Puts the free soul, which values every right,
> Through the excited blood's extravagance
> Into a mood which is its own despite.
> I thought it chance, more keenly looked—and then
> The wave stood still—and then rolled back again,
> Retiring from the target of its pride;
> But time comes round, renews the sport of tide.

MEPHISTOPHELES (*to the audience*):

> That's nothing new, not for the devil's ears;
> I've known it for a hundred thousand years.

FAUST (*continuing passionately*):

> Thus at a myriad points creeps up the sea,
> Infertile, spreading infertility;
> Now swells and grows and rolls and hides from sight
> The dreary strand, that tract of waste and blight.
> There wave on wave holds tyrant sway unfettered
> And then draws back—and nothing has been bettered;

And I could thus grow desperate to behold
This aimless power of elements uncontrolled.
But here my spirit dared a flight unknown:
Here could I war and, warring, win my throne.

And it is possible! The waves may swill,
They needs must fawn and cringe past every hill;
Whatever the bravado of its motion,
A slight height proudly towers against the ocean,
A slight depth draws it from its path designed.
Thus plan on plan came thronging to my mind—
Win for yourself, O Faust, this precious pleasure:
Lock out the lordly sea from shore and measure
A narrower measure for his briny plain,
Drive him far back into his own domain.
Thus step by step I argued and invented;
That is my wish, now dare to implement it!

(*Drums and martial music in the distance*)

MEPHISTOPHELES:

Perfectly simple! Hear those distant drums?

FAUST:

More war! A wise man's sorry when that comes.

MEPHISTOPHELES:

Oh—war or peace—what's wise is to take trouble,
To get one's pickings from such pots as bubble.
One waits and watches for each likely chance—
The chance has come! Faust, seize it and advance!

FAUST:

Don't pour such riddling nonsense in my ear!
Come to the point; what do you mean? Be clear!

MEPHISTOPHELES:

Upon my way here I got information
The emperor is plunged in consternation;
You know the good man. When we cut him capers
And falsified his purse with playful papers,

He would have bought the world, in truth.
For he was crowned while yet a youth
And liked to draw that false conclusion
That it's desirable and fine
And practicable to combine
Kingship and pleasure in collusion.

FAUST:

A great mistake! The man who is to rule
Must find in ruling his sole happiness;
A high will makes his breast a crowded school
But what he wills no man can plumb nor guess.
He hints to trusted ears a plan disguised
And it is done—and all the world surprised.
Thus will he always wear the highest crown
As worthiest of it—pleasure brings one down.

MEPHISTOPHELES:

Not so our man. 'Twas pleasure at the helm
For *him*, while anarchy dissolved his realm,
Where big and small showed hostile reciprocities
And brothers interchanged atrocities,
Fort against fort, town against town,
The guilds against the ermine gown,
The bishop fights his flock and dean—
And all are foes as soon as seen.
In churches blood and death; beyond the gate
Merchants and travellers meet a common fate.
And all grew brave—and to no small extent;
To live was self-defence—That's how it went.

FAUST:

It went, it limped, it fell, regained its feet,
Then toppled and fell rolling in the street.

MEPHISTOPHELES:

And none dared say things were not what they should be,
For each could be important—and each would be.
Even the smallest passed the test;
It got too mad at last though for the best.
The sound men rose, in arms, that this should cease,

And said: 'He is our lord who gives us peace.
The Emperor can't and won't—Let us elect us
A brand-new Emperor to resurrect us,
Who will secure each subject's right
And in a world made new and bright
Wed peace with justice to protect us.'

FAUST:

That sounds like priestcraft.

MEPHISTOPHELES:

Priests were in it too,
Watching their well-fed bellies got their due;
Yes, in it more than most, went doubles, trebles;
As the rebellion grew, they blessed the rebels.
And our old Emperor, whom we filled with mirth,
Comes here to fight—his last fight perhaps on earth.

FAUST:

I pity him; he was so good, so giving.

MEPHISTOPHELES:

Come, we shall see! Man shall have hope while living.
Let's free him from this narrow gorge below!
Once saved, he's saved a thousand times, you know.
Who knows if the dice may yet fall true?
If he have luck, he will have vassals too.

*(They cross the range and look down on the army in the valley. Drums
and military music)*

I see they've taken up a strong position;
We'll join them, then they're sure of their ambition.

FAUST:

But what is there to look for so!
Deceit? Enchantment? Hollow show.

MEPHISTOPHELES:

Why, what wins battles—craft of war!
But hold to your great scheme the more
And keep your mind upon your goal.

If we preserve the Emperor's throne and land,
Then you can kneel and take your dole—
The fief of all the boundless strand.

FAUST:

You have done much already. Now—
Now win a battle! Show me how!

MEPHISTOPHELES:

No, you shall win it, believe you me.
It's you to-day are C.-in-C.

FAUST:

You'd put me on a pretty peak—
Commanding in a tongue I cannot speak!

MEPHISTOPHELES:

Leave that to your General Staff! It's taken
They're there to save the Commander's bacon.
War's ordure I knew long before,
Now I've resolved to order war
With mountain manpower, old as earth;
Their general gets his money's worth.

FAUST:

Who're these, in arms, who come apace?
Have you stirred up the mountain race?

(*The Three Mighty Men step forward*)

MEPHISTOPHELES:

No, just these three who're drawing near.
You'll note, of very different ages,
And different clothes and weapons too they wear;
You'll find these fellows worth their wages.
(*to the audience*) To-day all children gaze with glee
On armour knightly or historic;
And, allegoric though my oafs may be,
They'll please the more *because* they're allegoric.

BASHER (*young*):

    When a chap looks me in the eye
    I promptly bash his kisser fit to blind him,
    And when the coward starts to fly
    I grab his hair that flies behind him.

GRABBER (*mature*):

    They're a sheer farce your empty broils,
    One wastes one's time with them at best;
    Be tireless raking in the spoils,
    Then you can ask for all the rest.

HOARDER (*elderly*):

    Small profit too in *your* exertion—
    Great wealth one moment, then dispersion,
    The stream of life sweeps it away.
    Taking is quite all right, it's better still to hold things;
    Let me, the grey-haired chap, control things—
    You'll not be robbed till Judgment Day.

THE BATTLEFIELD[1]

(Faust arrives, in armour, before the Emperor's tent. The Three Mighty Men follow him)

FAUST:

We come, Sire, hoping you have no objection;
For foresight, even uncalled for, bears inspection.
You know that the mountain folk have thoughts and tricks,
Have gone to school to nature and the rocks—

EMPEROR:

I understand, I credit what you say;
But, my good man, what use is this to-day?

FAUST:

Things have turned out just as the best desire
Who firm and loyal stand behind you, Sire.
The enemy comes, your soldiers burn to fight;
Now order your attack, the moment's right.

EMPEROR (*to his Commander-in-Chief*):

I here resign all claims to the command.
Prince, I confide your duty to your hand.

COMMANDER-IN-CHIEF:

Then forward our right wing! The enemy's left
Are coming up and this is their objective;
An abortive thrust—because our loyal troops
Young, fit, and tried, will make it ineffective.

FAUST:

Permit then that this merry hero may
Be enlisted in your ranks without delay,
And thus incorporated through and through
Among your troops exploit his might for you.

[1] The battle has been much condensed in this version.

BASHER (*stepping forward*):
>Who shows his face to me, he'll only turn it
>Away with both his jaws put through the mangle;
>Who turns his back, one blow leaves neck and head
>A loose repulsive mess to drip and dangle.
>And if your soldiers, while I rage,
>Go in with swords and clubs and down 'em,
>The enemy, man on man, will drop
>And their own blood will choke and drown 'em.

(*He goes out*)

COMMANDER-IN-CHIEF:
>Our centre phalanx! Move up gradually,
>Join action in full strength, but cautiously;
>Just on the right they're finding things expensive,
>Our weight of arms has shattered their offensive.

FAUST:
>Then order this man also to the fray!
>He's quick, whatever he meets he sweeps away.

GRABBER (*stepping forward*):
>To this brave army's blood and thunder
>Shall now be joined the thirst for plunder;
>And let each man's objective be
>The rival Emperor's grand marquee.
>He hasn't long for pride and dalliance;
>No, I myself will lead your big battalions.

QUICKLOOT (*Vivandière, clinging to him*):
>I'm not spliced up to him, I know,
>But he is still my dearest beau.
>We've such a harvest, such a catch!
>Women are savage when they snatch
>And ruthless when they rob, you see.
>Anything goes. Forward to victory!

(*They go out together*)

COMMANDER-IN-CHIEF:
>Upon our left, as was to be foreseen,
>They've thrown their right in force. Now man for man

Will meet this furious drive designed to take
The narrow gorge where victory is at stake.

FAUST:

Deign, Sire, to notice this man too. No wrong
Is done when someone strengthens what is strong.

HOARDER (*stepping forward*):

The left need feel no more depression!
My presence always guarantees possession.
Your target? This old man can hit it;
What I once hold, no bolt shall split it.

(*He goes out*)

MEPHISTOPHELES (*coming down from above*):

Now see how in the background yonder
From where the rock teeth gape asunder
Figures in armour forward forge
To pack the narrows of the gorge,
With helm and harness, shield and spear,
Forming a rampart in our rear,
Waiting their cue for battle, Sire.

(*aside*) But where they come from, don't inquire.
I've not been idle, should you doubt,
I've cleared the armouries round about;
On foot and horse they stood as though
They still were lords of earth, you know;
Upon a time knights, kings and kaisers—
And now just empty snailshells, hollow visors!
Many a phantom, dressed up so, engages
To play—and to the life—the Middle Ages.
Stuffed with whatever devilkins,
To-day this armour lives and wins.

(*loudly again*) Hark! They begin to show their mettle—
Tin pot colliding with tin kettle!
And by our standards tattered flags are waving,
They've waited long to satisfy this craving.
Mark well: an ancient race now holds this height,
Prepared and glad to fight a modern fight.

(*A dreadful peal of trumpets. The battle follows*)

FAUST:

> That hollow armour, brought from vaults to light—
> The open air restores its ancient might;
> Yonder it rattles, jangles, clanks around—
> A wonderful, unreal sound.

MEPHISTOPHELES:

> Quite right! They're now beyond all stopping;
> Hark to their knighthoods clouting, clopping,
> The good old days have found new life.
> Armlets and greaves are thronging thickly
> Like Ghibelline and Guelf and quickly
> Renew their never-ending strife.
> Firm in traditional detestation,
> Immune to reconciliation—
> And now the din is rank and rife.
> At last, as on all red-devil-days,
> You find that party hatred pays
> To the last horror known by men;
> Now sounds of contrapuntal panic
> With shriller notes in keys satanic
> Spread terror through the distant glen.

(The orchestra reaches a climax. The battle is won)

THE RIVAL EMPEROR'S TENT

(A throne and wealthy trappings)

QUICKLOOT:

We are the first ones here, you see.

GRABBER:

No raven flies as fast as we.

QUICKLOOT:

These heaps of treasure! What a crop!
Where can I start? Where can I stop?

GRABBER:

Look, this whole tent is crammed to burst!
I don't know what to seize on first.

QUICKLOOT:

I'd like this carpet for my own,
My bed is often hard as stone.

GRABBER:

Here hangs a steel mace, spike on spike,
I've long been looking for its like.

QUICKLOOT:

This scarlet cloak with golden seams—
I used to see it in my dreams.

GRABBER *(taking the weapon)*:

With such a mace the job's soon done,
One kills one's man and passes on.
Already found so much to pack?
Why, that's all rubbish in your sack.
No, leave that lumber where it lay,

Take one of these small chests away.
They hold the wages for the troops—
Pure gold within these iron hoops.

QUICKLOOT:

Oh but it is a murderous weight!
I cannot lift or shift it, mate.

GRABBER:

Then quick, bend down! Down! You won't crack.
I'll hoist it on your sturdy back.

QUICKLOOT:

Oh dear! Oh dear! You've done it, you!
This load is breaking me in two.

(*The treasure chest falls and bursts*)

GRABBER:

There lies the red gold in a heap—
Down on your knees and rake it up!

QUICKLOOT:

It will be still an ample measure—

(*An aide-de-camp enters*)

AIDE-DE-CAMP:

What are you doing in this sanctum,
Rummaging through the Emperor's treasure?

GRABBER:

You hired our limbs—that seemed to suit;
Now we collect our share of loot
From captured tents, as soldiers do;
And we, take note, are soldiers too.

AIDE-DE-CAMP:

No, among *us* that is not done—
Soldier and dirty thief in one!
Our Emperor welcomes no recruit
Who's not an honest man to boot.

GRABBER:

>Oh honesty! We know that game,
>Contribution is its name.
>You're all alike the way you live,
>The motto of your trade is 'Give!'
>We'll quit—and you, take what you've got!
>D'you think we're welcome here! We're not!

(*He goes out with Quickloot. The Emperor enters with his retinue*)

EMPEROR:

>So be it, magic or no! To-day we have won the battle,
>Through the flat plains the foe disperse like frightened cattle.
>Here stands the empty throne, the traitor's useless prize,
>Making the tent seem small, hung round with tapestries.
>We, guarded by our own true guards with veneration,
>Like a true Emperor wait the envoys of each nation;
>From every side glad tidings, as from heaven, pour down—
>Peace to our realm and glad allegiance to our crown.
>And even if some jugglings helped us as we struggled,
>'Twas for ourselves alone we fought, whoever juggled.
>The defeated fell—whom jeers will ever prick and prod,
>The victor in his triumph thanks and praises God.
>And all together join, unbidden—such their choice is;
>'We praise thee now, our God' pours from a million voices.
>Yet for the highest praise I look devoutly there
>Back into my own heart—which formerly was rare.
>A prince may waste his reign when youth's delights begin it,
>But years will make him heed the unforgiving minute.

ARCHBISHOP:

>Receive the heartfelt thanks of all men at this hour!
>You make us strong and sure, assuring your own power.

EMPEROR:

>And so I now dismiss you, that this glorious day
>Be spent in solemn thought; let each man think and pray.

(*The secular princes go out. Only the archbishop remains*)

ARCHBISHOP (*pathetically*):

>As chancellor I am gone, as bishop I stay here;

A warning, solemn spirit drives me to your ear.
In my paternal heart fear for your safety gnaws.

EMPEROR:

Fear in this hour of joy! Lord Bishop, for what cause?

ARCHBISHOP:

With what a bitter grief I find on this occasion
Your hallowed head in league with the Satanic persuasion!
True, it would seem, assured of your imperial hope—
Alas, in mockery of God and Father Pope;
Who, when he learns of this, will quickly overwhelm
With vengeful, sacred bolt you and your sinful realm.
But beat your breast; from what you have won in heaven's
      despite
Give back to Mother Church at once a moderate mite!
That broad hill district where you had your G.H.Q.,
Where evil spirits formed a league to rescue you
And your susceptible ear was lent the prince of lies,
Regenerate, grant that ground to sacred enterprise;
With mountains and thick woods, yes, right into the dis-
      tance,
With foothills green and lush to give our sheep subsistence,
And clear lakes rich in fish and brooks innumerable
Whose quick meanderings descend into the vale,
And the broad vale itself with fief and field and garden;
Let your contrition speak and you, Sire, shall find pardon.

EMPEROR:

My heavy fault has plunged my heart so deep in fright;
Take it and draw your own limits as you think right.

ARCHBISHOP:

First then that desecrate spot where sin contrived to unnerve
      us,
Proclaim it straightaway devoted to God's service!
So quickly in my mind I see strong walls aspire,
The glance of the rising sun already lights the choir,
The building grows, the transepts into a cross deploy,
The nave extends and towers to give believers joy
And, while in ardent faith they throng the lofty door,

Through hill and vale rings out a bell not heard before,
From the high towers it sounds, which force their way to
      heaven;
The penitents arrive to find their sins forgiven.
That day, so great—so near, pray God—of consecration
Will find your presence, Sire, its greatest decoration.

EMPEROR:

Aye! May this great work lead a pious congregation
To praise the Lord—and so give *me* my expiation.
Enough! I feel my soul already soars on high.

ARCHBISHOP:

As chancellor now, I ask one last formality.

EMPEROR:

A form of transfer . . . as the transferee defines it . . .
The Church. Come, give it here; the transferor gladly signs
      it.

(*The Archbishop has taken leave but turns back at the door*)

ARCHBISHOP:

Item: this work requires from you, Sire, as its betterer,
Your land-dues and in toto—tithes, rents, rates, etcetera,
For ever. It costs cash, its decent preservation,
And overheads attend careful administration.
Even to build it soon on such a desert site,
Out of your priceless loot requires a golden mite.
Moreover we shall need—I make, Sire, a clean breast of it—
Brought from a distance timber, lime, slates, all the rest of it.
Transport? The folk won't leave the pulpit in the lurch;
The church will bless the man who lives to serve the church.

(*He goes out*)

EMPEROR:

The sin that burdens me is heavy and extensive.
Yes, those damned sorcerers, I've found them most expen-
      sive.

(*The Archbishop returns once more, with the lowest possible obeisance*)

ARCHBISHOP:
>Excuse me, Sire. But you assigned that infamous man
>The seashore of the realm; he must expect our ban
>Unless, to prove repentance, you bestow there too
>On Holy Church all kinds and types of revenue.

EMPEROR (*peevishly*):
>But the land is not there, it lies leagues out at sea!

ARCHBISHOP:
>With right and patience time is all men's guarantee.
>We trust your word, we trust your strong hand at the helm.

(*He goes out*)

EMPEROR (*alone*):
>It would be simpler, perhaps, to sign away the realm.

ACT V

★

OPEN COUNTRY

WANDERER:

Aye! It's they, the shady lindens
Grown so old and yet so strong.
And I chance again to find them
After wandering so long!
Aye, it is the old place, truly;
There's the hut which sheltered me
Tossed upon those sand-dunes yonder
By the storm-distracted sea.
Worthy couple, quick to help me,
I would bless my hosts again.
Talk of meeting me to-day!
They were old already then.
Ah, but they were pious people!
Shall I knock? Or call? Well met,
If to-day, still hospitable,
They delight in good works yet!

BAUCIS (*a very old woman*):

Oh dear stranger! Softly! Softly!
Quiet! For my husband's sake!
Long sleep helps him to be active
In the short time he's awake.

WANDERER:

Mother, tell me, is it really
You? At last can man and wife
Now be thanked for what they once
Did to save a young man's life?
Are you Baucis, then so busy
To fill a half-dead mouth with food?

(*Her husband appears*)

Are *you* Philemon, then so sturdy
To save my treasures from the flood?
Yours the quickly kindled beacon,
Yours the silver-sounding bell,
The issue of that dread adventure
Was your trust—you bore it well.

And now let me walk out yonder,
Look upon the boundless sea—
There to kneel and pray; my heart
Feels so full, it troubles me.

(*He walks forward on to the dunes*)

PHILEMON (*to Baucis*):
Hurry now and lay the table
Where the garden flowers are bright.
Let him run and scare himself
When he can't believe his sight.

(*joining the Wanderer*) That which savaged you so fiercely—
Waves on waves in foaming spleen—
Here you see become a garden,
Altered to a heavenly scene.
Old by then, I could not lend
A helping hand as on a day,
And my powers had waned already
When the waves were far away.
Clever people's daring servants
Dug their dykes and dammed them high,
Whittling down the sea's dominion
To usurp its mastery.
Look! Green meadow after meadow,
Pasture, garden, village, wood.
But the sun is almost setting,
Come and eat—you'll find it good.
Aye, far off there sails are moving
Towards sure harbour for the night.
Birds, you know, they know their nest—
That is now the harbour site.
Gazing now into the distance

First you find the sea's blue seam—
All the spaces left and right
Thick with folk and houses teem.

BAUCIS:

Aye, it *is* a marvel happened;
It still gives me qualms to-day.
For the way it all was done—
It was not a proper way.

PHILEMON:

Can the Emperor have sinned
Granting him that fief of strand?
Did a herald with a trumpet
Not proclaim it round the land?
Their first foothold it was planted
Near our dunes, not far from here,
Tents and huts—but soon a palace
In green meadows must appear!

BAUCIS:

In vain the workmen's daily racket—
Pick and shovel, slog and slam;
Where the flames by *night* were swarming,
Stood next day a brand new dam.
Human victims must have bled,
Night resounded with such woe—
Fireflakes flowing to the sea;
Morning a canal would show.
Godless man he is, he covets
This our cabin and our wood;
To this overweening neighbour
Everyone must be subdued.

PHILEMON:

All the same we have his offer—
Fine new property elsewhere.

BAUCIS:

Do not trust that water-surface;
On your upland—stand you there!

PHILEMON:

> Let us move on to the chapel,
> There to watch the last of day.
> Trusting in our father's God
> Let us ring the bell and pray!

PALACE

(*Extensive formal garden; broad canal, straight as a ruler. Faust, in
the depths of old age, walking about and brooding*)

LYNCEUS THE WATCHMAN (*through a megaphone*):
> The sun is sinking, the last ships
> Are sailing blithely into port.
> A fair-sized bark on the canal
> Will reach us soon, its way is short.
> Her coloured pennants flutter gaily,
> Ready to dock her masts are bare;
> On you the skipper rests his hopes
> And luck now answers all your prayer.

(*The little bell rings out on the dunes*)

FAUST (*with a start*):
> Oh that damned ringing! All too shameful
> It wounds me like a stab in the back;
> Before my eyes my realm is endless,
> Behind—I'm vexed by what I lack,
> Reminding me with spiteful ringing
> My great possessions are not sound.
> The linden plot, the wooden cabin,
> The crumbling church are not my ground.
> And, should I wish to rest me yonder,
> Strange shadows fill my heart with fear—
> Thorn in the eyes and thorn in the foot;
> Oh were I far away from here!

LYNCEUS (*as above*):
> The gay-rigged bark, how merrily
> A sharp breeze bears it to the quay!

How, as it speeds, it towers on high—
Chests, crates and sacks to reach the sky!

(*The ship docks, laden with foreign merchandise. Mephistopheles
and the Three Mighty Men lead the chorus*)

SAILORS' CHORUS:

Here we land!
Oh here we are!
Luck to the owner
From afar!

(*They come ashore and the goods are unloaded*)

MEPHISTOPHELES:

You see how we have earned our bays!
Content to win the owner's praise.
We went out with two ships, no more,
And we're in harbour with a score.
Our cargo'll prove, to those who doubt,
What great things we have brought about.
The free sea makes the spirit free;
Who thinks of thinking on the sea?
The sea demands quick nerve and grip,
You catch a fish, you catch a ship,
And starting in command of three
You hook a fourth one presently.
Ill omen for the fifth ship? Quite.
Given the might, you have the right.
One asks the What and skips the How.
No need to know much navigation;
War, trade and piracy are one
Inseparable combination.

THE THREE MIGHTY MEN:

Not thank nor greet!
Not greet nor thank!
As if he found
Our cargo stank!
He makes a most
Offensive face;
Our royal freight
Is in disgrace.

MEPHISTOPHELES:

> You need not wait for
> More reward!
> You had your share
> While still on board.

THE THREE MIGHTY MEN:

> Oh that was but
> To lighten toil,
> We all demand.
> An equal spoil.

MEPHISTOPHELES:

> First, room by room.
> Arrange up there
> The precious cargo—
> Nothing spare!
> When Faust comes in
> To such a sight
> And reckons all,
> Of it aright,
> He'll surely not
> Be stingy then,
> He'll feast the fleet
> And feast again.
> To-morrow the painted birds are due,
> I'll see the best results ensue.

> *(The cargo is removed)*

MEPHISTOPHELES (*to Faust*):

> With brow austere, with frowning glance
> You greet your latest vast advance.
> Crowning your high sagacity,
> Your shore is reconciled to sea;
> The sea agrees to take your ships
> Out from your shore on rapid trips;
> Admit then: from your palace here
> Your arms embrace the earthly sphere.
> From here we started on this track,

Here stood your first poor wooden shack;
A little ditch was scratched in dirt
Where now the busy rudders spurt.
Your lofty mind, your navvies' worth,
Obtained for prize the sea and earth.
From here moreover—

FAUST:

This damned Here!
It's that which makes my spirits drear.
I must confess to you, the expert,
It sears my heart with flame on flame,
I find I can no more endure it!
And, while I say so, I feel shame.
That aged couple should have yielded,
I want the lindens in my grip,
Since these few trees that are denied me
Undo my world-wide ownership.
Yonder I planned a panorama,
A platform built from bough to bough,
To grant my eye a distant prospect
Of all that I have done till now,
Whence I could see at once aligned
The masterpiece of human mind,
Which energizes skilfully
The peoples' lands reclaimed from sea.

Hence is our soul upon the rack
Who feel, midst plenty, what we lack.
That clanging bell, that linden-scent,
Are like a tomb—I feel so pent.
The omnipotence of random will
Is broken on this sandy hill.
How to shake off this thing which binds me!
The bell rings out—and fury blinds me.

MEPHISTOPHELES:

Naturally. Such a nagging pain
Must fill your life with gall, it's plain
To everyone. Your cultured ear
Must find this tinkling vile to hear.

And that damned ding-dong rising high
Befogs the happy evening sky,
Mingling in all things that befall
From baptism to burial,
As if between that ding and dong
Life were a dream that had gone wrong.

FAUST:

That obstinacy, all-perverse,
Makes all one's finest gains a curse,
So that, though gnawed at heart, one must
At last grow tired of being just.

MEPHISTOPHELES:

Why then these scruples? Your vocation
Has long meant shifts of population.

FAUST:

Then go and shift them me at once!
You know the pretty little place
That I envisaged in their case.

MEPHISTOPHELES:

One takes hem out and dumps them—Why,
Before one knows, they're up and spry;
A fine new homestead, in due course,
Atones them for our use of force.

(*He whistles shrilly. The Three re-enter*)

The owner's orders! Come! Don't sorrow,
For there's a seamen's feast to-morrow.

THE THREE MIGHTY MEN:

The old man welcomed us like beasts;
It's what he owes us—he-men's feasts!

MEPHISTOPHELES (*to the audience*):

A tale long past is told again;
There was a Naboth's vineyard then.

DEEP NIGHT

LYNCEUS (*singing on the watch-tower*):

> For seeing begotten,
> My sight my employ,
> And sworn to the watch-tower,
> The world gives me joy.
> I gaze in the distance,
> I mark in the near
> The moon and the planets,
> The woods and the deer.
> So find I in all things
> Eternal delight,
> The more that they please me
> Am pleased to have sight.
> Oh eyes, what has reached you,
> So gladly aware,
> Whatever its outcome,
> At least it was fair.

> But not only to have pleasure
> Am I posted on this tower;
> What a gruesome horror threatens
> From the world at this dark hour!
> Glancing sparks I see in fountains
> Through the lindens' double night.
> Burrowing onward, fanned by breezes,
> Ever stronger glows the light.
> Ah! The hut, once damp and mossy,
> Flames within it pave and lave it;
> There's a call for quick assistance,
> No one is at hand to save it.
> Ah, that aged decent couple,
> Once so careful about fire,
> Smothered now in smoke and cinders!
> What an end! How strange! How dire!

Blaze on blaze and glowing red
Stands that black and lichened frame;
Could the good folk but escape
From that hell of crazy flame!
Little lightnings, tonguing, twisting,
Climb through leaf and bough, insisting;
Dried-up branches burn and flicker—
One quick flare and down they fall.
Must my eyes bear this? Must I be
So far-sighted after all?
Now the little church collapses
Under falling bough on bough.
In a swirl of pointed flames
The tree-tops are on fire by now.
To their roots the hollow tree-trunks
Glow, empurpled in their glow.

      (*Long pause. Chanting*)

That which once enticed my vision—
Gone like ages long ago!

FAUST (*on the balcony, towards the dunes*):
      What is this whimpering above me?
      Both words and burden are too late.
      My watchman wails; my heart resents
      An action so precipitate.
      Yet, though the lindens' life be ended
      In half-charred trunks, a thing to dread,
      One soon can build there a gazebo
      To gaze on the unlimited.
      There I see too that fine new dwelling
      Which will enfold that aged pair,
      Who grateful for my generous forethought
      Can spend their last days blithely there.

MEPHISTOPHELES AND THE THREE MIGHTY MEN (*below*):
      At a full gallop, riding strong,
      Excuse us if our task went wrong.
      We knocked and beat upon the door
      But no one opened it the more;

We went on knocking, rattled it,
The rotten door gave way and split;
We shouted angry threats at once
But still we met with no response.
And, as in such a case holds good
They could have heard us if they would;
But we refused to make delay,
We quickly dragged them both away.
The pain they felt was only slight,
They fell down dead at once from fright.
A stranger hidden in the hut,
Who wished to fight, we knocked him out.
And in that short but savage fight
The scattered fire-coals set alight
Some straw. And that unbridled fire
Now gives all three one funeral pyre.

FAUST:

Did you then turn deaf ears to me?
I meant exchange, not robbery.
That random stroke, so wild, perverse—
I curse it; you can share the curse.

CHORUS:

The word rings out, the ancient word:
When violence speaks, she's gladly heard.
Only be brave and tough, then take
House, goods—and self—and lay your stake.

(*They go out*)

FAUST (*on the balcony*):

The stars conceal their light and now
The fire sinks down and glimmers low;
A shivery breeze still fanning it
Covers me here with smoke and grit.
Quickly required, too quickly done—
What shadowy shapes come drifting on?

MIDNIGHT

(Four Grey Women approach)

WANT:

They call me Want.

DEBT:

They call me Debt.

CARE:

They call me Care.

NEED:

They call me Need.

DEBT:

The door is locked and we cannot get in.

NEED:

Nor do we want to, there's wealth within.

WANT:

That makes me a shadow.

DEBT:

That makes me naught.

NEED:

The pampered spare me never a thought.

CARE:

My sisters, you cannot and may not get in.
But the keyhole there lets Care creep in.

(Care vanishes)

WANT:

      Come, grey sisters, away from here!

DEBT:

      Debt at your side as close as fear.

NEED:

      And Need at your heels as close as breath.

THE THREE:

      Drifting cloud and vanishing star!
      Look yonder, look yonder!
              From far, from far,
      He's coming, our brother, he's coming . . .
              Death.

FAUST (*in the palace*):

      Where four came hither, but three go hence;
      I heard them speak, I could not catch the sense.
      An echoing word resembling 'breath'—
      And a dark rhyme-word followed: 'Death'.
      A hollow, muffled, spectral sound to hear.
      Not yet have I fought my way out to the air.
      All magic—from my path if I could spurn it,
      All incantation—once for all unlearn it,
      To face you, Nature, as one man of men—
      It would be worth it to be human then.
      As I was once, before I probed the hidden,
      And cursed my world and self with words forbidden.
      But now such spectredom so throngs the air
      That none knows how to dodge it, none knows where.
      Though one day greet us with a rational gleam,
      The night entangles us in webs of dream.
      We come back happy from the fields of spring—
      And a bird croaks. Croaks what? Some evil thing.
      Enmeshed in superstition night and morn,
      It forms and shows itself and comes to warn.
      And we, so scared, stand without friend or kin,
      And the door creaks—and nobody comes in.
      Anyone here?

CARE:

> The answer should be clear.

FAUST:

> And you, who *are* you then?

CARE:

> I am just here.

FAUST:

> Take yourself off!

CARE:

> This is where I belong.

> (*Faust is first angry, then recovers himself*)

FAUST (*to himself*):
> Take care, Faust, speak no magic spell, be strong.

CARE:

> Though to me no ear would hearken,
>> Echoes through the heart must darken;
>> Changing shape from hour to hour
>> I employ my savage power.
> On the road or on the sea,
> Constant fearful company,
> Never looked for, always found,
> Cursed—but flattered by the sound.
> Care? Have you never met with Care?

FAUST:

> I have only galloped through the world
> And clutched each lust and longing by the hair;
> What did not please me, I let go,
> What flowed away, I let it flow.
> I have only felt, only fulfilled desire,
> And once again desired and thus with power
> Have stormed my way through life; first great and
>> strong,
> Now moving sagely, prudently along.

This earthly circle I know well enough.
Towards the Beyond the view has been cut off;
Fool—who directs that way his dazzled eye,
Contrives himself a double in the sky!
Let him look round him here, not stray beyond;
To a sound man this world must needs respond.
To roam into eternity is vain!
What he perceives, he can attain.
Thus let him walk along his earthlong day;
Though phantoms haunt him, let him go his way,
And, *moving on*, to weal and woe assent—
He, at each moment ever discontent!

CARE

Whomsoever I possess,
    Finds the world but nothingness;
    Gloom descends on him for ever,
    Seeing sunrise, sunset, never;
    Though his senses are not wrong,
    Darknesses within him throng,
    Who—of all that he may own—
    Never owns himself alone.
    Luck, ill luck, become but fancy;
    Starving in the midst of plenty,
    Be it rapture, be it sorrow,
    He postpones it till to-morrow,
    Fixed upon futurity,
    Can never really come to be.

FAUST:

Stop! You cannot touch me so!
Such nonsense I refuse to hear.
Away! Your evil tale of woe
Could fog a wise man's brain, however clear.

CARE:

Let him come or go—he'll find
    That he can't make up his mind;
    Half-way down his destined way
    Starts to stumble, grope and sway,
    Ever deeper lost and thwarted,

Seeing all things more distorted,
Burden to himself and others,
Who takes breath and, breathing, smothers;
If not smothered, yet not living,
Not revolted, not self-giving.
Endless round—he must pursue it:
Painful Leave-it, hateful Do-it,
Freedom now, now harsh constraint,
Broken sleep that leaves him faint,
Bind him to his one position
And prepare him for perdition.

FAUST:

You outcast phantoms! Thus a thousand times
You lead the human race into illusion;
Even indifferent days you thus transform
To nets of torment, nightmares of confusion.
Demons, I know, are hardly shaken off,
Their ghostly gripping bonds man cannot sever;
But you, O Care, your power that creeps and grows—
I shall not recognize it ever.

CARE:

Then feel it now! As, leaving you,
This final curse on you I cast.
The human race are blind their whole life through;
Now, Faust, let *you* be blind at last.

(*She breathes upon him*)

FAUST (*blinded*):

The night seems pressing in more thickly, thickly,
Yet in my inmost heart a light shines clear;
What I have planned, I must complete it quickly;
Only the master's word is weighty here.
Up and to work, my men! Each man of you!
And bring my bold conception to full view.
Take up your tools and toil with pick and spade!
What has been outlined must at once be *made*.
Good order, active diligence,
Ensure the fairest recompense;
That this vast work completion find,
A thousand hands need but one mind.

GREAT FORECOURT OF THE PALACE

(Torches)

MEPHISTOPHELES *(leading the way, as foreman)*:
> Come on, come on! Come in, come in!
> You gangling gang of Lemurs,
> You half-alives patched up with thin
> Sinews and skulls and femurs.

LEMURS *(in chorus)*
> You call us, here we are at hand;
> And, as we understand it,
> We stand to win a stretch of land
> Intended as our mandate.
>
> Our pointed staves we have them here,
> Our chain to measure sections,
> But why you called on us, we fear,
> Has slipped our recollections.

MEPHISTOPHELES:
> Artistic efforts we can spare;
> And just let each one's nature guide him!
> Let now the longest lie his length down there,
> You others prise away the turf beside him;
> As for your forebears long asleep,
> Dig you an oblong, long and deep.
> To narrow house from palace hall
> Is such a stupid way to end it all.

(The Lemurs begin to dig, with mocking gestures)

LEMURS:
> When I was young and lived and loved,
> Methought it was passing sweet;

In the merry rout and roundabout
There would I twirl my feet.

But sneaking Age has upped his crutch
And downed me unaware;
I stumbled over the door of the grave—
Why was it open *there*?

FAUST (*groping his way from the palace*):
Oh how this clink of spades rejoices me!
For that is my conscripted labour,
The earth is now her own good neighbour
And sets the waves a boundary—
Confinement strict and strenuous.

MEPHISTOPHELES (*aside*):
And yet you've only toiled for *us*
With all your damming, all your dyking—
Spreading a feast to Neptune's liking
To glut that water-demon's maw.
In all respects you're lost and stranded,
The elements with us have banded—
Annihilation is the law.

FAUST:
Foreman!

MEPHISTOPHELES:
Here!

FAUST:
Use every means you can;
Bring all your gangs up and exhort them—
Threaten them if you like or court them—
But pay or woo or force each man!
And day by day send word to me, assessing
How my intended earthworks are progressing.

MEPHISTOPHELES (*half aloud*):
The word to-day, from what I've heard,
Is not 'intended' but 'interred'.

FAUST:

A swamp along the mountains' flank
Makes all my previous gains contaminate;
My deeds, if I could drain this sink,
Would culminate as well as terminate:
To open to the millions living space,
Not danger-proof but free to run their race.
Green fields and fruitful; men and cattle hiving
Upon this newest earth at once and thriving,
Settled at once beneath this sheltering hill
Heaped by the masses' brave and busy skill.
With such a heavenly land behind this hedge,
The sea beyond may bluster to its edge
And, as it gnaws to swamp the work of masons,
To stop the gap one common impulse hastens.
Aye! Wedded to this concept like a wife,
I find this wisdom's final form:
He only earns his freedom and his life
Who takes them every day by storm.
And so a man, beset by dangers here,
As child, man, old man, spends his manly year.
Oh to see such activity,
Treading free ground with people that are free!
Then could I bid the passing moment:
'Linger a while, thou art so fair!'
The traces of my earthly days can never
Sink in the aeons unaware.
And I, who feel ahead such heights of bliss,
At last enjoy my highest moment—this.

(*Faust sinks back; the Lemurs seize him and lay him on the ground*)

MEPHISTOPHELES:

By no joy sated, filled by no success,
Still whoring after shapes that flutter past,
This last ill moment of sheer emptiness—
The poor man yearns to hold it fast.
He who withstood me with such strength,
Time masters him and here he lies his length.
The clock stands still—

CHORUS:

> Stands still! Like
> > midnight ... silent ... stilled.
>
> Its hand drops down.

MEPHISTOPHELES:

> Drops down; it is fulfilled.

LEMURS:

> It is gone by.

MEPHISTOPHELES:

> Gone by! A stupid phrase.
> Why say gone by?
> Gone by—pure naught—complete monotony.
> What use these cycles of creation!
> Or snatching off the creatures to negation!
> 'It is gone by!'—and we can draw the inference:
> If it had *not* been, it would make no difference;
> The wheel revolves the same, no more, no less.
> I should prefer eternal emptiness.

INTERMENT

LEMUR SOLO:

> Oh who has built the house so ill
> With spade and shovel rough?

LEMUR CHORUS:

> For you, dull guest in hempen garb,
> Yon house is fine enough.

LEMUR SOLO:

> No chair or table in the hall—
> Who's furnished it so meagre?

LEMUR CHORUS:

> The loan was only for a time;
> The creditors are eager.

MEPHISTOPHELES:

> Here lies the corpse and if the soul would flee
> At once I show the bond, the blood-signed scroll;
> Though now, alas, they have so many means
> To cheat the devil of a soul.
> Our old procedure gives offence,
> Our new has not yet found endorsement;
> Once I'd have managed it alone,
> Now I must look for reinforcement.
> Come up, you devils! Make it double quick!
> You straight-horned peers and crooked-horned as well,
> You old and sterling devil-stock,
> Come up—and bring with you the jaws of Hell!

> *(The Jaws of Hell open upon the left)*

> The eye-teeth gape; the throat's enormous vault
> Spews forth a raging fiery flow

And through the smoking cyclone of the gullet
I see the infernal city's eternal glow.
You do right well to make the sinner quake;
And yet they think it all a dream, a fake.
Now, devils, watch this body! How does it seem?
See if you see a phosphorescent gleam.
That is the little soul, Psyche with wings—
Pull out her wings and it's a noisome worm;
With my own seal I'll set my stamp upon her,
Then forth with her into the fiery storm!
Come, claw and comb the air, strain every nerve
To catch her though she flutter, though she swerve.
To stay in her old lodging gives her pain;
The genius is about to leave the brain.

(*Glory, from above, on the right*)

THE HOST OF HEAVEN:

Fly, as directed,
Heaven's elected,
Serenely whereby
Sin shall have pardon,
Dust become garden;
Stay your progression,
Make intercession,
Trace for all natures
A path to the sky.

MEPHISTOPHELES:

Discords I hear, a filthy strumming tumbling
Down from the sky with the unwelcome day;
That is the angels' boyish-girlish fumbling,
Their canting taste *likes* it to sound that way.
You know how we, in hours of deep damnation,
Have schemed annihilation for mankind;
Those angels use for adoration
The greatest stigma we could find.
They come so fawningly, the milksops!
They've kidnapped many souls before our eyes,
They fight us back with our own weapons;

They too are devils—in disguise.
Defeat to-day would mean disgrace eternal;
So stand around the grave and stand infernal!

CHORUS OF ANGELS (*scattering roses*):
>   Roses, you glowing ones,
>   Balsam-bestowing ones!
>   Fluttering peaceably,
>   Healing invisibly,
>   Spraylets to glide upon,
>   Budlets unspied upon,
>   Hasten to bloom!
>
>   Green and empurpled,
>   Spring must have room;
>   Carry your heaven
>   Into the tomb!

MEPHISTOPHELES (*to the Satans*):
>   Why duck and squirm? Is that our wont in hell?
>   Stand fast and let them strew their roses!
>   Each gawk to his post and guard it well!
>   With such small flowers the enemy proposes
>   To snow up overheated devils;
>   Why, at your breath it melts and shrivels.
>   Now puff, you blow-fiends!
>
>   ... Here! Stop! Stop!
>   Your reek is bleaching the whole flight and crop.
>   Don't blow so hard! Muzzle your chops and noses!
>   I'll swear you've *over*blown those roses!
>   You never know when you have passed the turn!
>   They're more than shrunk—they're browned, they're
>   dry, they *burn*!
>   Bright flames of poison pelt on us already;
>   In close formation, devils! Steady! Steady!
>   What! All your valour gone! Your strength burns low!
>   The devils sense a strange insidious glow.

CHORUS OF ANGELS:

> Blooms of pure blessedness,
> Flames of pure joyfulness,
> Love is their ministry,
> Rapture their legacy,
> All we could pray.
> Hosts of eternity
> Find in such verity
> Heavens of clarity,
> Aeons of day!

MEPHISTOPHELES:

> A curse upon these louts! How scurvy!
> My Satans are all topsy-turvy
> And turning cartwheels in their path
> And tumbling arse-up into Hell.
> I hope you like your well-earned sulphur bath!
> I stand my ground and wish you well.

> (*He beats off the roses falling around him*)

CHORUS OF ANGELS:

> What is not right for you
> You must beware it,
> What does despite to you
> You may not bear it.
> Lightnings may dart on us,
> We must have heart in us.
> Lovers can only be
> Rescued by love.

MEPHISTOPHELES:

> My head's aflame! Liver and heart aflame!
> A super-devilish element!
> Hell's fires to this are damped and tame.
> That's why you make such wild lament,
> You luckless folk in love, despised alas,
> Who sprain your necks to watch your sweethearts pass.

> Me too! What draws my head in that direction?
> I, their sworn enemy! Is this defection?
> To see them once was agony or worse.

Has something alien entered me completely?
To see their flower of youth affects me now so sweetly;
I want to curse them—but what chokes the curse?
And, if I let them now befool me,
Whom can the future call a fool?
These dashing fellows, though I hate them,
Inspire a longing that I cannot rule.
Beautiful children, must I not infer
That you like me are kin to Lucifer?
With every look you seem more fair, more fair.
Oh come near, angels, glance on me! Come near!

ANGEL:

See, we approach—why do you shrink away?
We come; if you can face us—why, then, stay!

(*The Angels, closing in, occupy all the space*)

CHOIR OF ANGELS:

Flames of dear feeling,
Rise beyond seeing!
Self-condemned being—
Truth be its healing!
Blessed transition
Forth from perdition,
Into Eternity,
Into the One!

MEPHISTOPHELES (*collecting himself*):

Look! The damned flames are out that caused my fall.
Now I become myself and curse you one and all!

CHOIR OF ANGELS:

Light of Creation!
Whom it embraces
Finds all the graces
Found in salvation.
Praising in unison
Rise to your goal!

Purged is the air now—
Breathe now the soul!

(*They soar up, carrying away the immortal part of Faust*)

MEPHISTOPHELES (*looking around him*):

But how is this? Where have they moved away to?
You juveniles, to take me by surprise!
Flying off heavenwards—and with my prey too;
They nibbled at this grave to win this prize.
Wresting from me a great and matchless treasure,
That noble soul which gave me right of seizure
They've filched by throwing rose-dust in my eyes.
Who is there now to lend an ear to
My wrong, restore my hard-earned right?
You have been hoaxed—so late in your career too—
It's your own fault, you're in a lurid plight.
Such gross mismanagement—outrageous!
Such a great outlay squandered! Oh the shame!
Erotic folly, vulgar lust, contagious
To an old devil at the game!
Experience has indulged its appetite
On such a childish-foolish level;
When all is said, the folly is not slight
Which in the end has seized the devil.

MOUNTAIN GORGES

*(Forest, Rock, Wilderness. Holy anchorites, disposed here and there,
at different heights among the chasms)*

CHORUS AND ECHO:
>   Woods clamber tremblingly,
>   Crags bear down weightily,
>   Roots cling tenaciously,
>   Trunks make a density;
>   Spurting of wave on wave—
>   Deep lies our hermits' cave.
>   Lions around in dumb
>   Friendliness gently come,
>   Honour our sanctuary,
>   Love's holy privacy.

PATER ECSTATICUS *(floating up and down)*:
>   Rapture which yearns ever,
>   Love-bond which burns ever,
>   Pain in me seething up,
>   Love of God foaming up.
>   Arrows, pierce through me and,
>   Lances, subdue me and,
>   Clubs, leave no form in me,
>   Thunderstorms, storm in me!
>   That now the Nothingness
>   Drown all in emptiness,
>   One constant star must shine,
>   Kernel of love divine.

PATER PROFUNDUS *(from the depths)*:
>   As at my feet a craggy chasm
>   Weighs on a deeper chasm's prop,

As streams in thousands flow and sparkle
Towards the dread rapids' foaming drop,
As with its own strong urge the tree-trunk
Climbs up the air, erect and tall,
Even so is that almighty love
Which all things forms and fosters all.

Around me here a frantic rushing
Makes wood and cleft a stormy sea,
Yet full of love the water's fullness
Roars as it plumbs the cavity,
Ordained to straightway feed the valley;
The thunderbolt which crashed in flame
To cleanse the air which bore within it
Poison and evil mists, these same

Are messengers of love, announcing
What round us ever moves and makes.
May that light kindle too within me
Where the cold spirit gropes and quakes,
Self-racked in body's bonds of dullness,
Riveted fast in chains that smart.
O God, have mercy on my thoughts,
Give light to my impoverished heart!

PATER SERAPHICUS (*at a middle height*):
What a morning cloudlet hovers
Through the pine-trees' waving hair!
I divine what lives within it—
Newborn souls are gathered there.

CHORUS OF BLESSED BOYS:
Tell us, Father, where we wander,
Tell us, good one, who we are!
All of us are happy, living
In a state that naught can mar.

PATER SERAPHICUS:
Innocents—who, born at midnight
With half-opened soul and brain,
Were at once your parents' loss,

Were at once the angels' gain.
That a living man is present,
That you feel, so draw you near!
Though earth's rugged ways are barred you,
Alien to your happy sphere.
Climb up then into my eyes—
Organ matching world and earth;
See this region, using mine
For the eyes you lost at birth.

(*He takes them into himself*)

Those are trees—and those are crags—
See that river plunging deep,
Which with its enormous welter
Delves a passage, short though deep.

BLESSED BOYS (*from inside him*):
Yes, that is a mighty prospect—
But too sad this world below,
Shaking us with fear and horror.
Reverend father, let us go!

PATER SERAPHICUS:
Aye. Ascend to higher circles,
Ever grow invisibly
As God's presence makes you stronger
Through eternal purity.
It is this which feeds the spirit,
Rules the heights of revelation:
Window into love eternal
Opening upon salvation.

BLESSED BOYS (*circling round the highest peak*):
Joyfully gyring
Dance ye in union,
Hands linked and choiring
Blessed communion!
Pattern before you,
Godly, to cheer you,
Whom you adore, you
Soon shall see near you.

ANGELS (*floating in the higher air, carrying the immortal part of Faust*):
Saved, saved now is that precious part
Of our spirit world from evil:
'Should a man strive with all his heart,
Heaven can foil the devil.'
And if love also from on high
Has helped him through his sorrow,
The hallowed legions of the sky
Will give him glad good morrow.

THE YOUNGER ANGELS:
Ah those roses, *their* donation—
Loving-holy penitent women—
Helped us to defeat Apollyon,
Brought our work to consummation,
To this priceless spirit's capture.
Devils, as we scattered rapture,
Struck by roses, fled in panic,
Feeling not their pains Satanic
But the pains of love's disaster;
Even that old Satan-master
Felt a torment arrowed, marrowed.
Alleluia! Hell is harrowed.

THE MORE PERFECT ANGELS:
This scrap of earth, alas,
We must convoy it;
Were it asbestos, yet
Earth would alloy it.
When soul's dynamic force
Has drawn up matter
Into itself, then no
Angel could shatter
The bonds of that twoness—
The oneness that tied it;
Eternal love alone
Knows to divide it.

THE YOUNGER ANGELS:

> Close, round the mountain top,
> To my perceiving
> Moves like a mist a
> Spiritual living.
> Those clouds are turning bright,
> I see a sainted flight:
> Children unmeshed from
> Meshes of earth, they
> Fly in a ring,
> Being refreshed from
> Heaven's rebirth they
> Bask in its spring.
> Faust, to begin to rise
> Towards highest Paradise,
> With them must wing.

THE BLESSED BOYS:

> Gladly receiving this
> Chrysalid entity,
> Now we achieve, in this,
> Angels' identity.
> Let the cocoon which is
> Round him be broken!
> Great! Fair! How soon he is
> Heaven-awoken!

DOCTOR MARIANUS (*in the highest, purest cell*):

> Here is the prospect free,
> Spirit-uplifting.
> Yonder go women's shapes
> Over me drifting;
> And, wreathed in her seven
> Bright stars, they attend her—
> The high queen of Heaven;
> I gaze on her splendour.

> (*Entranced*)

> Highest empress of the world,
> Let these blue and sacred

Tents of heaven here unfurled
Show me now thy secret!
Sanction that which in man's breast
Soft and strong prepares him—
Love which joyful, love which blest
Towards thy presence bears him.

Thine august commands are such,
Nothing can subdue us—
Fires burn gentler at thy touch
Should thy peace imbue us.
Virgin, pure as none are pure,
Mother, pearl of honour,
Chosen as our queen, the sure
Godhead stamped upon her!

Light clouds enlacing
Circle her splendour—
These are the penitent
Women, a tender
Race. At thy knee,
Sipping the air, they
Call upon thee.

Thou, albeit immaculate,
It is of thy fashion
That the easily seduced
Sue to thy compassion.

Such whom frailty reft, are hard,
Hard to save, if ever;
Who can burst the bonds of lust
Through his own endeavour?
Do not sliding gradients cause
Sudden slips? What maiden
Is not fooled by flattering glance,
Tokens flattery-laden?

(*The Mater Gloriosa floats into vision*)

CHORUS OF PENITENT WOMEN:

> Mary, in soaring
> To kingdoms eternal,
> Hear our imploring
> Thou beyond rival!
> Fount of survival!

MAGNA PECCATRIX:

> By my love which mingled tears with
> Balm to bathe His feet, revering
> Him thy son, now God-transfigured,
> When the Pharisees were jeering;
> By that vessel which so sweetly
> Spilt its perfumed wealth profusely,
> By my hair which dried those holy
> Limbs, around them falling loosely—

MULIER SAMARITANA:

> By the well where Father Abram
> Watered once his flocks when marching,
> By the bucket once allowed to
> Touch and cool Christ's lips when parching;
> By that pure and generous source which
> Now extends its irrigation,
> Overbrimming, ever-crystal,
> Flowing through the whole creation—

MARIA AEGYPTIACA:

> By that more than sacred garden
> Where they laid the Lord to rest,
> By the arm which from the portal
> Thrust me back with stern behest;
> By my forty years' repentance
> Served out in a desert land,
> By the blessed word of parting
> Which I copied in the sand

THE THREE:

> Thou who to most sinning women
> Thy dear presence ne'er deniest,

Raising us repentant women
To eternities the highest,
Make to *this* good soul concession—
Only once misled by pleasure
To a never-dreamt transgression;
Grant her pardon in her measure.

ONE OF THE PENITENTS (*formerly named Gretchen*):
Uniquely tender,
Thou queen of splendour,
Thy visage render
Benign towards my felicity!
My love of old, he
Is now consoled, he
Comes back to me.

BLESSED BOYS (*approaching, flying in circles*):
Passing beyond us
So soon in resplendence,
He will make ample
Return for our tendance;
Early we left the
Terrestrial chorus;
He will instruct us,
Instructed before us.

THE SINGLE PENITENT (*formerly named Gretchen*):
By choirs of noble souls surrounded
This new one scarcely feels his soul,
Can scarcely sense this life unbounded,
Yet fills at once his heavenly role.
See how he sheds the earthly leaven,
Tears off each shroud of old untruth,
And from apparel woven in heaven
Shines forth his pristine power of youth!
Mary, grant me to instruct him,
Dazzled as yet by this new day.

MATER GLORIOSA:

> Come then! To higher spheres conduct him!
> Divining *you*, he knows the way.

DOCTOR MARIANUS (*bowing in adoration*):

> All you tender penitents,
> Gaze on her who saves you—
> Thus you change your lineaments
> And salvation laves you.
> To her feet each virtue crawl,
> Let her will transcend us;
> Virgin, Mother, Queen of All,
> Goddess, still befriend us!

CHORUS MYSTICUS:

> All that is past of us
> Was but reflected;
> All that was lost in us
> Here is corrected;
> All indescribables
> Here we descry;
> Eternal Womanhead
> Leads us on high.

FINIS

Translated by Louis MacNeice

CUTS

As stated in the introduction, this version of *Faust* was primarily intended for broadcasting. The original text (Part I and II together) runs to more than twelve thousand lines. This seemed too much for the air —and too much not only in quantity. In cutting about a third of the whole, our first aim was to bring out the character and story of Faust himself while, negatively, we decided to sacrifice such passages as seemed irrelevant or inferior or merely obscure. In taking this liberty with a great master we were reassured by the remembrance that he himself had intended (an intention never realized) to cut this work into shape. Our cuts are as follows (the numbering of the lines being that of the *Editiones Helveticae*):

PART I

Lines 1–32 (*Zuegnung*) and 33–242 (*Vorspiel auf dem Theater*).
726–9 and 731.
808–27, 842–51, 949–80 (condensing the Holiday Scene).
1042–7.
1627–34.
1835–49, 1868–2050. It was with regret that we sacrificed the Student but, as far as radio was concerned, we felt it was high time that Faust got started on his travels.
2073–336 (the scene in Auerbach's Cellar). We cut the whole of this not only because it is unsuitable for broadcasting but because, for all its fame, it seems comparatively dull and because, logically and dramatically, the *Hexenküche* makes a better opening for Faust's 'new course of Life'.
2388–401, 2416–28, 2448–68, 2475–80, 2540–66, 2585–6, 2591–2. The Witch's Kitchen, like Auerbach's Cellar, depends largely on visual effects. I accordingly not only condensed this scene but slightly reshuffled the order of speeches. I have here partly restored the order but kept my omissions.
2695–709. I could not stomach Faust's sentimentalizing over Gretchen's chair.

3664–9, 3671–2, 3714–5.

3968–73, 3978–85, 4072–95, 4136–75, 4210–22. The Walpurgisnacht seems to cry out for pruning. The Proktophantasmist, for instance, can mean little now to a listener—or even to a reader.

4223–394. The Walpurgisnachtstraum, as a quite irrelevant digression and anticlimax, is completely cut except for its last four lines which follow naturally from Mephistopheles' 'Nur immer diese Lust zum Wahn!' The prose scene which follows has been slightly shaved down.

PART II

The cuts here are much more drastic than in Part I. As was to be expected. While everyone agrees that Part II is incoherent, I am not of those who find all its incoherences profound.

Act I

4947–6030. We took out the whole Carnival as distracting attention from Faust and throwing this Act out of balance.

6063–82.

6401–2.

Act II

6583–5.

6683–818. I cut the Baccalaureus as Baccalaureus because in Part I I had cut him as Student.

7080–151. The Classical Walpurgisnacht needs pruning even more than its Gothic counterpart. Goethe here sowed with the whole sack so that it is hard to see his myth for his mythology.

7187–8, 7214–48.

7406½–10½, 7451–4, 7463–8.

7503–824. I here cut the Earthquake, the Ants and Pygmies, and—more regretfully—the baiting of Mephistopheles by the Lamiae, etc.

7873–948 (the latter part of the discussion between Thales and Anaxagoras).

7951–8033 (Mephistopheles' encounter with the Phorkyads, more usually known as the Graiae). The point of this lies in Mephistopheles' transformation into a Phorkyad which was not required in our radio version as we intended to cut the first part of Act III.

8058–77, 8168–226.

8275–312 (The Telchines of Rhodes) and 8355–423 (the Psylli, Marsi, Dorides, etc.). Some fine lyrical passages were hereby sacrificed but we did not wish to lose sight of Homunculus.

Act III

8488–9126. This great and drastic cut was made not only for the sake of lucidity and a tighter continuity but because this translator has a blind spot for the *Helena* in general and because, incidentally, Goethe's 'classical' verse is more difficult to translate than his rhyming verse. And it seemed both convenient and arresting to start in front of Faust's Castle.

9419–561 (Menelaus' unconvincing offensive).

9578–9, 9590–7, 9607–19, 9629–94, 9790–862. Whatever his effect in German, Euphorion threatened to prove embarrassing in English or even unintentionally comic. Hence this pruning.

9955–10038. This cut afforded a good transition to Act IV.

Act IV

10071–94, 10101–23, 10126–7. Here, as often, we dispensed with some of Goethe's geology.

10160–76, 10321–2.

10345–422, 10427–36, 10439–96, 10571–763. This battle was too much to cope with. The passages retained do justice, we hope, to Goethe's satirical intentions.

10811–16, 10833–48, 10859–63, 10871–950, 10953–73. The Emperor's bestowing of awards on his Big Four seemed boring—and an anti-climax.

10987–90.

Act V

11107–10.

11620–35, 11640–4, 11648–53, 11656–8, 11164–670, 11672. The Bosch-like grotesquerie of the passages here cut seemed too likely to spoil the effect of the scenes which precede and follow.

11741–4, 11771–5, 11780–800, 11809–14. By the same reasoning I abridged Mephistopheles' lust, so saving him some of his dignity.

THE GERMAN LIBRARY
in 100 Volumes

All volumes available in hardcover and paperback editions at your bookstore
or from the publisher. For more information on The German Library write
to: The Continuum Publishing Company, 370 Lexington Avenue, New York,
NY 10017.